GW01607774

WHO WERE THEY?

QUESTION & ANSWER ENCYCLOPEDIA

WHO WERE THEY?

General Editor Lesley Firth

KINGFISHER BOOKS

First published in 1985 by Kingfisher Books Limited
Elsley Court, 20-22 Great Titchfield Street
London W1P 7AD

BRITISH LIBRARY CATALOGUING IN PUBLICATION DATA

Who Were They?—(Question and Answer encyclopedia)
1. Biography—Juvenile literature
I. Firth, Lesley II. Series
920′.02 CT107
ISBN 0-86272-145-8
D. L. TO: 897-1985

Phototypeset by Crawley Composition Ltd, Crawley, Sussex

Colour separations by Newsele Litho Ltd, Milan Italy

Printed in Spain by Artes Gráficas Toledo, S.A.

Editor
Bridget Daly

Authors
Neil Ardley
Brenda Clarke
Jean Cooke
Mark Lambert
James Muirden
Theodore Rowland-Entwistle
Jenny Vaughan
Brian Williams

Artists
Norma Burgin/John Martin & Artists
Mark Bergin/Temple Art
Paul Crompton/John Martin & Artists
Geraint Derbyshire/John Martin & Artists
Jim Dugdale/Jillian Burgess
John James/Temple Art
Jerry Malone/Tudor Art
Bernard Robinson/Tudor Art
Mike Roffe
Mike Saunders/Jillian Burgess

CONTENTS

WORLD HISTORY

SCIENCE AND TECHNOLOGY

MYTHS, LEGENDS AND HEROES

THE ARTS AND ENTERTAINMENT

MEDICINE

OUT IN SPACE

EXPLORERS AND PIONEERS

WORLD HISTORY

▼WHO LIVED AT UR?

Ur was one of the city states built by the ancient Sumerians. Its ruins lie in southern Iraq.

The Sumerians founded Ur during the 3000s BC. The River Euphrates flowed nearby.

The early settlement at Ur was wiped out by a flood. It is remembered in the Bible as the Great Flood.

A highly civilized group of Sumerian people settled at Ur after the Flood. They included sculptors, potters, metalworkers and builders.

A royal graveyard, containing gold, silver and bronze objects dating from about 2700 BC was excavated in the 1920s.

The kings and queens of Ur were buried with a large retinue of their poisoned courtiers who hoped to serve them in the next world.

▼WHO WAS SARGON OF AKKAD?

Sargon was a king who reigned from about 2630 to 2305 BC. He founded the world's first major empire.

Sargon was vizier (chief minister) to one of the kings who ruled in Sumer (modern Iraq). He took over the throne and founded the city of Agade (or Akkad), somewhere in north Babylonia.

In time he conquered all the other kings of Sumer, extending his rule south to the Persian Gulf, west to the Mediterranean and north into what is now Turkey.

The people of this empire were called Akkadians.

Under Sargon's successors the Akkadians developed the art of writing. They also designed the first helmets to be used in warfare, made out of copper and leather.

▼WHO WERE THE HITTITES?

The Hittites had an empire based on what is now central Turkey. It lasted for about 700 years, from the 1900s to the 1200s BC.

The Hittites were related to the peoples of Europe and northern India. They crossed the Caucasus mountains from east-central Europe to conquer Anatolia (modern Turkey). Their capital was the city of Hattusas near modern Ankara.

After they became powerful around 1500 BC the Hittites spread south along the Mediterranean coast.

They wrote on clay tablets, both in hieroglyphics (picture writing) and in cuneiform (wedge-shaped) script. Hittite kings also served as high priests. They had a legal system. The Hittites were among the first people to use iron.

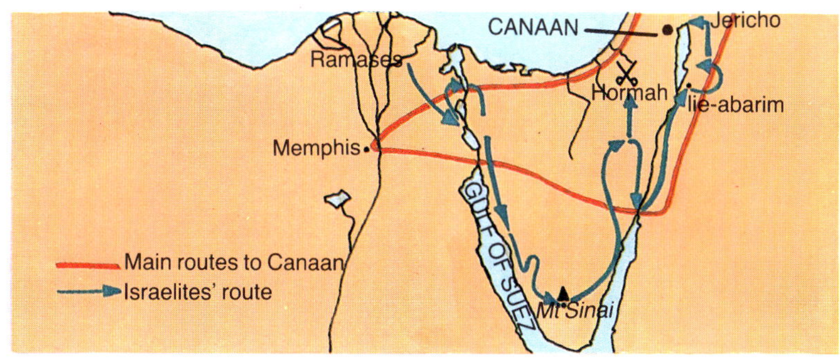

▲ WHO WAS MOSES?

Moses was the Hebrew prophet who led the people of Israel from bondage in Egypt to Canaan.

The story of Moses is told in four books of the Bible – *Exodus*, *Leviticus*, *Numbers*, and *Deuteronomy*. This is the only direct reference to him.

However, an Egyptian inscription of about 1200 BC mentions Israel, and an Egyptian historian, Manetheo, writing in the 200s BC, told how certain Hebrews were expelled from Egypt. 'Moses' used to be an Egyptian name.

According to the Bible account, the Israelites were an oppressed group in Egypt, which provided slave labour. Moses became their leader and led them out of Egypt towards Canaan (Palestine), probably during the 1200s BC.

For many years the Israelites were nomads (wanderers). They did not reach Canaan until after Moses's death.

► WHO WERE THE ASSYRIANS?

The Assyrians lived in the northern part of what is now Iraq. They flourished from about 2900 BC to 600 BC.

The Assyrians lived in a highland area on the Tigris River. Their chief cities were Assur and Nineveh. Their buildings were made of sun-baked bricks, but their temples and palaces had stone foundations and elaborate stone wall-carvings.

The Assyrian state was built up around its army, the first large force to be equipped with iron weapons. The Assyrians had an empire stretching from Egypt to the Persian Gulf.

They extracted silver from mines in what is now southern Turkey, and Assur soon became a thriving trade centre between east and west. Small rods of silver were used in exchange for goods (especially fabrics, horses and camels).

The Assyrians worshipped Ashur, god of war. In 600 BC Assyria was conquered by the Medes and Babylonians.

► WHO WAS KING NEBUCHADREZZAR?

Nebuchadrezzar was king of Babylon from 605 to 562 BC. In the Bible his name is spelt Nebuchadnezzar.

A few months before he succeeded his father Nebuchadrezzar took Syria and Palestine from Egypt in a battle at Carchemish, now in Southern Turkey.

The Egyptians encouraged the defeated peoples to rebel, so Nebuchadrezzar had to mount a series of fresh campaigns. He overran the little Hebrew kingdom of Judah, sacked its capital, Jerusalem, and took many captives to Babylon.

Babylon was already a big and wealthy city when Nebuchadrezzar became king, and he added many fine buildings to it, including the Ishtar Gate (right).

To please his wife, Amytis, who disliked the flat plain of Babylon, Nebuchadrezzar built a huge terraced garden, famed as the Hanging Gardens of Babylon and one of the Seven Wonders of the World.

◀ WHICH KING FIRST UNITED EGYPT?

Menes, the ruler of Upper Egypt, conquered the Nile Delta area (Lower Egypt) in about 2850 BC.

The kingdom of Upper Egypt extended south from where Cairo is now to the first cataract (steep rapids) on the Nile, the site of present-day Aswan.

Menes wore a white, cone-shaped crown. The rulers of Lower Egypt, the swampy area of the delta, wore a red crown. After his conquest, Menes wore a double crown, the white crown inside the red one.

Menes was a personal name. He took a different name as a ruler, and appears in lists of early kings as Narmer, Lord of the Two Lands.

The king built a capital city for his double kingdom at Memphis, south-west of Cairo. Its citadel was surrounded by a white wall.

Egyptian history tells us that Menes/Narmer reigned for 62 years and that his wife's name was Neith-hetep. Soon after he died – killed by a hippopotamus – he was declared a god.

▶ WHO SENT A TRADING EXPEDITION TO THE LAND OF PUNT?

Many Egyptian rulers sent traders to the Land of Punt, but the two most famous expeditions were sent by Mentohotep III and Queen Hatshepsut.

The Land of Punt lay on the Red Sea Coast, now occupied by part of Ethiopia, Djibouti and north Somalia. It was rich in gold, ivory and spices.

Early trading between Egypt and Punt was apparently overland. By about 2000 BC, the third king Mentohotep decided that it would be better to go by sea and sent one ship.

About 500 years later Queen Hatshepsut, who ruled from 1503 to 1482 BC, sent a fleet of five ships to Punt. An inscription in her mortuary temple at Deir el-Bahri, near Luxor, describes the cargo of fragrant woods, incense, eye make-up, apes, dogs, panther-skins and living myrrh trees.

▶ WHO DESIGNED THE FIRST PYRAMID?

The first pyramid was the Step Pyramid at Saqqara in Egypt. It was designed by Imhotep, physician to King Djoser, in the 2500s BC.

Imhotep is notable as the first non-royal person whose name is recorded in history.

He was a man who had many talents. As well as being the court physician, he was a priest, an astronomer, a writer and the king's chief minister.

The Step Pyramid is about 60 metres high. It was the central feature of Djoser's royal tomb. The tomb was more than just a burial place. It provided temples, galleries, courtyards and rooms where religious services could be held to honour the dead king.

The whole Saqqara complex was the first monument to be built entirely of stone: mud bricks were usually used for part or all of the buildings.

The Step Pyramid is so called because its sides form a series of giant steps. Later pyramids had smooth sides.

▼ WHICH PHARAOH WORSHIPPED ONE GOD?

Amenhotep IV, who reigned from 1379 to 1362 BC, worshipped the Aten, the Sun's disc.

Amenhotep IV became pharaoh (king) on the death of his father, whose reign was peaceful and prosperous.

Early in his reign the young pharaoh adopted the worship of the Aten. He believed the Aten was the God of the whole world, not just of Egypt. He abolished the worship of Amun-Rê, a combined god of the air and god of the Sun, and a host of other gods and goddesses. He took the name Akhenaten after the Aten.

Akhenaten built a new capital city, Akhetaton, abandoning Thebes, the city of his predecessors.

Akhenaten devoted all his time to religious affairs and neglected the government of his country, so by the time he died, at the age of about 30, Egypt had lost most of its empire. Soon Egypt returned to its old gods, and Thebes became the capital once more.

▲ WHO WAS NEFERTITI?

Nefertiti was the wife of Akhenaten, the Egyptian pharaoh who tried to change his country's religion.

Nefertiti may have been a foreign princess, but she and her husband looked so alike that she may well have been his sister. Egyptian kings often married their sisters.

We know what Nefertiti and Akhenaten looked like because several sculpted heads of the couple were found in the ruins of Akhenaten's capital, Akhetaton, a site now called Tell el-Amarna.

During Akhenaten's reign, artists were encouraged to make lifelike portraits rather than the stylized types that are typical of art in ancient Egypt.

Nefertiti helped her husband in his religious ceremonies and bore him six daughters. Then she seems to have fallen out of favour and lived in retirement or maybe even in captivity.

Nefertiti's eldest daughter, Meritaten, married Akhenaten's successor, Smenkhkare.

▼ WHO WAS TUTANKHAMUN?

Tutankhamun was the young son-in-law of Akhenaten. His tomb, containing rich treasures, was found in 1922.

Tutankhamun's original name was Tutankhaten. He was married as a boy to Akhenaten's third daughter, Ankhesenpaaten. He was probably only about ten years old when he was made pharaoh in succession to Smenkhkare, his wife's brother-in-law.

After about two years the boy-king proclaimed that all the old gods should be worshipped again and he moved back to the old capital city, Thebes. He also changed his name to incorporate that of the god Amun-Rê.

Tutankhamun's tomb, found in 1922 by the British archaeologist Howard Carter, is the only Egyptian royal tomb that had escaped being robbed in ancient times. The King's body still lies in the tomb, but most of the treasures are in the Cairo Museum. Tutankhamun was only 18 when he died in 1351 BC.

▼WHO WERE THE JOMON PEOPLE?

The Jomon people were the earliest known inhabitants of Japan. They lived from about 7000 BC to 250 BC.

'Jomon' means 'cord pattern', and the Jomon people have been given their name because they made pottery with a cord pattern on it.

It seems likely that the Jomon people came to Japan from Siberia. They may be the ancestors of the Ainu, a small group of people living in northern Japan. The Ainu men have bushy hair and beards, unlike most modern Japanese.

The Jomon people lived in semi-underground houses, pits covered with sloping roofs. They used stone tools. They appear to have lived largely by hunting and fishing.

Large middens (rubbish dumps) have been found containing the remains of shellfish with bone fish hooks which were apparently used for deep-sea fishing. So the Jomon people must have had sea-going boats. Bones show that they ate wild boar and deer.

▲WHICH EMPERORS WERE KNOWN AS THE SONS OF HEAVEN?

The title 'Son of Heaven' was given to Chinese emperors from Bronze Age times until the title of emperor was abolished in 1911.

The early rulers of China were both emperors and high priests. The rulers of the Shang Dynasty (family) who ruled from 1766 BC, claimed to be descended from a supreme god named Shang Ti.

The Shang believed that the emperor was their link with heaven and that when he died he would go there to join Shang Ti. During an emperor's lifetime he was also known as the 'One Man'.

For many hundreds of years the Chinese worshipped the spirits of their ancestors; the 'Son of Heaven' was the leader of this religious cult.

The title 'Son of Heaven' may have originated before the Shang Dynasty. But the earlier dynasties, going back to 2697 BC, are largely legendary and nothing definite is known about them.

▲WHO WAS LAO-TSE?

Lao-tse was a philosopher who lived in China about 2,500 years ago. He founded a religion and way of thinking called Taoism.

According to tradition, Lao-tse was born in 604 BC. His name was actually Lao-tan, but he is called Lao-tse which means 'Master Lao'. At first he lived a quiet, secluded life which grew busier after he became librarian at the court of the Chou dynasty of Chinese rulers.

Lao-tse became known for his wisdom and philosophy and in 517 BC the young Confucius came to ask his advice.

Eventually Lao-tse tired of worldly affairs, and set out on a journey westward in search of rest and contemplation.

On his travels he met a warden at a frontier post with whom he left his writings on Tao, literally 'The Way'. He was last heard of journeying towards the Pass of Hsien-ku, in the western mountains of China.

Taoism advocates a simple, virtuous life, close to nature.

▲WHO WAS THE BUDDHA?

The Buddha, which means 'The Enlightened One', was Siddhartha Gautama, the son of an Indian prince who lived in the 500s BC. He spent most of his life preaching.

Tradition says that Siddhartha was born in 563 BC. He was brought up to a life of luxury. When he was 16 he married the Princess Yasodhara, and they had a son, Rahula.

When he was about 29 the prince realised that the world was full of sickness and misery. One night he left home, exchanged his rich clothes with the rags of a beggar and became a wandering monk.

For six years he tried to find enlightenment (religious understanding) by fasting and self-denial. He finally realised this was not the way either; he needed something in between riches and starvation.

Sitting under a Bo-tree one day to meditate, enlightenment suddenly came to him. He spent the rest of his life teaching others the way to *Nirvana* or happiness, by following the 'Middle Way'. He died at the age of 80.

▲WHO WAS CONFUCIUS?

Confucius was a Chinese philosopher who lived nearly 2,500 years ago. Millions of people have followed his teachings almost as a religion.

The real name of Confucius was K'ung Ch'iu. He became known as K'ung-fu-tzu, which means Great Master Kung; Confucius is a Latin form of that title.

Confucius was born in 551 BC in the town of Ch'ü-fou in Shantung province, where his descendants still live. He became famous as a scholar while still a young man.

Many people in China were poor, miserable and badly governed. Confucius believed in treating people as he would want to be treated. His ambition was to obtain a high government post so that he could put his ideas of peace and justice into practice. Eventually the rulers of his own state, Lu, gave him an apparently high post – but he soon found that he had no real power so he resigned to spend his last years teaching. He died at the age of 72.

▼WHO WERE THE NOK PEOPLE?

The Nok people lived from about 900 BC in what is now northern Nigeria. They were the earliest people in Black Africa to make sculptures.

Archaeologists first found the Nok sculptures in 1931. They are named after the little village of Nok which lies south-east of the town of Kano.

The art and way of life of these unknown people is called the Nok culture. Traces of it have been found at many other sites in the area north of the junction of the Niger and Benue rivers.

The sculptures are made of earthenware. Some are life-size human heads. Others are small models of animals and humans. All the human heads have pierced ears, so the people must have worn jewellery.

The Nok people also smelted iron and made stone axes. From the sculptures it seems that they were farmers.

Nobody knows how the Nok culture ended, but the present-day Yoruba tribe may be descended from the Nok.

▼WHO WAS SOCRATES?

Socrates was a leading philosopher and teacher in ancient Greece. His views have influenced people through the ages.

Socrates was born in Athens in 470 BC, the son of a sculptor and a midwife. He served in the Athenian army where he was commended for his courage in battle.

He was married to a woman named Xanthippe who was said to be very bad-tempered. Possibly she was annoyed because Socrates had no personal ambition and was not interested in money.

However, Socrates was at one time president of the Assembly, a sort of parliament of all Athenian citizens. There he made himself unpopular by resisting an illegal move to bring some generals to trial.

Socrates spent most of his time teaching young people his ideas of truth and virtue. His enemies accused him of corruption and heresy. As a result he was sentenced to die by drinking hemlock, a poison.

▲WHO WAS PLATO?

Plato was a writer and philosopher, the friend and pupil of Socrates. He was born in Athens in 427 BC.

Plato was born into a wealthy aristocratic family. At the age of 20 he became a pupil of Socrates.

After Socrates' death in 399 BC Plato spent some years travelling. Then he returned to Athens where he founded a school of science and philosophy (the two subjects were closely related in ancient Greece).

The school was held in a grove of olive trees sacred to a legendary hero, Academus. The school became known as the Academy; this name has been used for schools ever since.

He spent some time in Sicily, where he tried to train the ruler of Syracuse, Dionysius II, in philosophy.

In his writings Plato was able to describe the teaching of Socrates, who left no books of his own, as well as his own philosophy. He died in Athens at the age of 80.

▲WHO WAS ARISTOTLE?

Aristotle was the most important thinker of ancient Greece. He was employed for six years as tutor to Alexander the Great.

Aristotle's father was court doctor to Alexander's grandfather, Amyntas II. Aristotle himself went to Athens in 367 BC when he was 18 and studied at Plato's Academy for 20 years.

After his time in Macedonia as tutor to Alexander, Aristotle returned to Athens where he started his own school, the Lyceum. The buildings included a covered walk, the *peripatos*, and this is why Aristotle's college is often called the *peripatetic school*.

About a year before he died Aristotle had to flee from Athens because his enemies accused him of a lack of reverence for the gods.

Aristotle's writings on a wide range of subjects were rediscovered by European scholars in the later Middle Ages. His works were regarded as second only to the Bible in importance.

▲WHO WERE THE SPARTANS?

Sparta was a city-state of ancient Greece. Its citizens, the Spartans, were renowned for their military skill and their ability to do without luxuries.

The city lay in southern Greece, in the peninsula of Peloponnesos. Its people were divided into three groups. The Spartans were the aristocrats, trained as warriors, who owned the land.

A second group of Greeks, living under Spartan rule, were called *perioikoi*. They existed by trading which was forbidden to the true Spartans. The third group were the *helots*, or slaves, who farmed the Spartans' land for them and had few rights.

Spartan boys were taken from their mothers at the age of seven. They were trained by the State, mainly in gymnastics and the use of weapons. Men were not allowed to marry until they were 30.

Spartan girls also had gymnastic training, and gained considerable independence when grown up.

▲WHO WERE THE ETRUSCANS?

The Etruscans were the most important people in Italy before the ancient Romans. They lived in Etruria which is now known as Tuscany.

Nobody has yet been able to find out where the Etruscans came from or the details of their history.

The Etruscans have left a great many inscriptions but written in a language that no one has been able to read.

They built up a powerful empire in north-western Italy, becoming the first kings of Rome. They traded by sea with other places around the Mediterranean.

Most of our knowledge of the Etruscans comes from the works of art they left. They were skilled sculptors, in terracotta (a kind of pottery) and bronze. They also worked in iron, made beautiful jewellery and decorated their tombs with paintings.

The Etruscan empire was at its height in the 500s BC. It was absorbed by the Romans in the 300s BC.

▼WHO WERE THE PLEBEIANS OF ROME?

The plebeians, or plebs as the Romans called them, were the common people of Rome.

Rome had four classes of people: the patricians, or aristocracy, who had all the privileges and power; the plebs, freeborn citizens with little power; freedmen, former slaves with slightly fewer privileges than the plebs; and slaves, with few rights of any kind.

In the early days of the Roman Republic, in the 500s BC, the plebeians were unable to hold any public office, become priests or marry into patrician families. However, they could, and did, serve in the army.

Over a period of 200 years the plebeians won various rights. The most important was the right to elect their own tribunes, ten officials who could reject unfair decisions by magistrates. By 287 BC, the plebeians had won the right to join in lawmaking and to become priests.

▶ WHO WAS JULIUS CAESAR?

Gaius Julius Caesar was a brilliant Roman general and writer who became the ruler of Rome.

Caesar was a member of an aristocratic Roman family. He was born in 100 BC.

In 68 BC Caesar entered a political career, holding a succession of public positions. In 59 BC he was elected consul.

With two other men, Gnaeus Pompeius and Marcus Crassus, Caesar formed a three-man group to rule Rome, called the Triumvirate. After his year of office as consul Caesar went off to conquer Gaul (France). In nine years of campaigning he managed to evict the Germans who ruled Gaul and also to invade Britain twice.

In 49 BC Caesar returned to Rome and made himself dictator. He campaigned in Egypt where he fell in love with its queen, Cleopatra.

Although he ruled Rome wisely, he had enemies who were jealous of his success. In 44 BC they assassinated him.

◀ WHO WAS CLEOPATRA?

Cleopatra VII was the ruler of Egypt from 51 BC to 30 BC. She was beautiful and ruthless.

Cleopatra was the last of the Ptolemy family from Macedonia, who ruled Egypt for 300 years. On the death of her father in 51 BC she became joint ruler with her younger brother Ptolemy XIII who, in accordance with Egyptian tradition, also became her husband. She was then 18.

In 49 BC Ptolemy's guardians ousted Cleopatra from power. Then she met Julius Caesar, in Egypt pursuing his rival Pompey. Caesar put her back on the throne.

Ptolemy XIII having died, Cleopatra married a still younger brother, Ptolemy XIV, but went off to Rome with Caesar, and had his son.

After Caesar's death she returned to Egypt where she fell in love with another Roman general, Marcus Antonius. By him she had twins. When Antonius died, Cleopatra killed herself.

▶ WHO FOUNDED THE ARMENIAN EMPIRE?

The founder of the Armenian Empire was Tigranes the Great, who became king of that country in 95 BC.

Armenia was a region covering the present-day Armenian Soviet Socialist Republic and part of neighbouring Turkey.

Tigranes, sometimes called Dikran, came to the throne when he was about 45. At that time he was the hostage of a neighbouring king but he bought his freedom by handing over part of Armenia.

He began at once to enlarge his kingdom by attacking Parthia where he had been a hostage. In the next few years he overran Syria, northern Mesopotamia (now a good part of Iraq) and Phoenicia, now part of Lebanon and Israel.

Tigranes' expansionist policies brought him into conflict with Rome. An army led by Gnaeus Pompeius defeated him in 66 BC. Tigranes had to surrender and become a Roman vassal. His empire had vanished.

◀ WHO WAS JESUS OF NAZARETH?

Jesus was a Jewish rabbi (teacher) who founded the Christian religion. Its followers believe that he was the Son of God, sent to Earth to save mankind.

Jesus was born in Bethlehem in Judea, where his mother, Mary, and her husband Joseph, a carpenter, had travelled to register their names in a census. But his hometown was Nazareth in the province of Galilee.

Little is known about Jesus's early life, except that his parents fled to Egypt for a while to escape persecution by the king of Judea, Herod the Great. Herod ruled Judea for the Romans.

Jesus began teaching when he was about 30 years old. He soon had a large following of Jews who hailed him as the Messiah, a saviour whom prophets had said would come to help them.

The Romans and orthodox Jewish religious leaders saw Jesus as a troublemaker and he was tried and crucified in AD 29.

▶ WHO BECAME THE FIRST POPE?

According to tradition, the first pope, or head of the Christian Church, was Peter, one of the apostles (close followers) of Jesus of Nazareth.

Before he met Jesus, Peter's name was Simon. He was a fisherman. Jesus called him Peter, which means 'rock', saying 'Upon this rock I will build my Church'.

After Jesus was crucified in AD 29 he appeared to his disciples. Peter took the lead in proclaiming that Jesus had conquered death and was undoubtedly the Messiah (Christos in Greek).

Peter travelled, preaching the message of Jesus. Tradition has it that he went to Rome and became Bishop of Rome – the official title of popes ever since. He was martyred in about AD 64 in the reign of Emperor Nero.

A shrine, believed to have marked the grave of Peter, has been found under St Peter's Basilica in the Vatican in Rome.

▼ WHO WAS THE FIRST CHRISTIAN MISSIONARY?

The apostle Paul was the first true missionary. He preached Christianity to the Gentiles – that is, to non-Jewish peoples.

Paul was a Jewish tent-maker, named Saul, born in Tarsus in Asia Minor (modern Turkey). Having studied the Jewish religion in Jerusalem, Saul was shocked by the apparent new 'heresy' taught by Jesus, and set to work to wipe it out. As he was travelling from Jerusalem to Damascus he had a vision which convinced him that he was wrong; instead he became an ardent follower of Jesus. He is always regarded as an apostle, though his conversion came after Jesus's death.

Although a Roman citizen (Paul was the Latin form of his name), he did more than anyone else to spread Christianity. He was probably tried and put to death in Rome about AD 67 because of his revolutionary ideas.

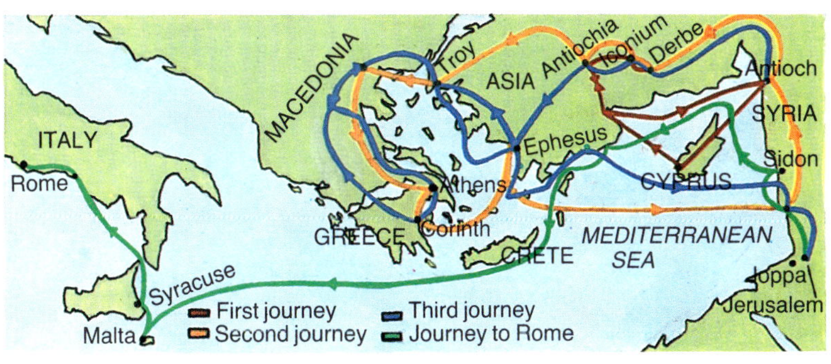

▶ WHO WERE THE SCYTHIANS?

The Scythians were a group of nomadic (wandering) tribes living in Scythia, the southern part of what is now the Soviet Union, more than 2,000 years ago.

The original homeland of the Scythians was around the Altai Mountains in Central Asia. They began moving westward about 800 BC, and by 650 BC they had conquered northern Iran and eastern Turkey.

The Medes of Persia drove the Scythians out. They then settled in what is now southern Russia and in the Crimea.

Some Scythians also moved into eastern Europe, as far west as Hungary and Poland. They were finally conquered by Goths in the AD 100s.

The Scythians were bold warriors, skilled archers and horsemen. Their graves contain fine sculptures and utensils in gold, silver and other metals. Some tombs in the Altai Mountains were found to be frozen, their contents preserved as in a modern deep-freeze.

▶ WHO WERE THE THRACIANS?

The Thracians were tribesmen who lived in the eastern part of the Balkan peninsula. Thrace now forms part of Greece, Turkey and Bulgaria.

Some Thracians in ancient times were warlike while others were peaceful farmers. They are first recorded more than 3,500 years ago.

They appear to have been fond of poetry and music. Their culture apparently influenced that of Greece, notably in religion.

The Thracians believed in life after death. They indulged in animal worship and human sacrifice. Among their important gods was Sabazius, who was similar to the Greek god Dionysus, god of vegetation and later god of wine.

The Greeks built many cities along the coast of Thrace. From the 300s BC the land was largely under Greek control. For a time in the 500s BC it was conquered by Persia. Byzantium (now Istanbul) was a Thracian city.

▶ WHO WERE THE CELTS?

The Celts were a group of tribes living in central Europe in the 500s BC. Many migrated west. Their language survives in Welsh, Gaelic and Breton.

Present-day descendants of the Celts are found in Brittany, Cornwall, Ireland, the Isle of Man and Scotland. The Cornish and Manx languages have almost died out. Because the Ancient Britons were Celts, many English place names are of Celtic origin.

In their heyday the Celts were both mighty warriors and good farmers. Many of their settlements were in huge hill forts, whose great earth ramparts can still be seen.

Celtic laws and traditions were not written down but passed on by word of mouth. They were preserved by the mysterious Druids, who were the religious leaders. The Druids held ceremonies among sacred groves of trees where they worshipped several gods, especially the Sun.

Celtic smiths worked in gold, bronze and iron.

▼WHO WAS ATTILA?

Attila was the leader of the Huns, a warlike group of tribes from central Asia which terrorized Europe in the AD 400s.

In AD 434 Attila and his brother Bleda became joint rulers of the Huns, at that time based in Hungary. After 11 years Attila murdered Bleda, so becoming sole ruler. In 447 he began a career of conquest.

He forced the rulers of the Eastern Roman Empire to pay him a large annual fee to leave them alone. He then led a large army of Huns into Gaul (France) and demanded the hand of Honoria, sister of the Western Roman emperor Valentinian III, in marriage. One story says that Honoria asked him to come so that she could escape from someone that she was unwillingly engaged to.

The Romans defeated Attila at Châlons-sur-Marne in 451. He died two years later.

▲WHO WAS QUEEN BOUDICA?

Boudica – often wrongly called Boadicea – was ruler of the Iceni, a Celtic British tribe, in about AD 60.

The queen became leader of the Iceni when her husband Prasutagus died, leaving her alone with her two daughters. Their kingdom was in what is now Norfolk, in East Anglia.

The Roman rulers in Britain maintained that Prasutagus had left his kingdom to the Roman emperor. When Boudica claimed the throne the Roman procurator (ruler), Decianus Catus, ordered her to be whipped. The soldiers who carried out the order also assaulted Boudica's daughters.

Led by their tall, red-headed queen, the Iceni tribe at once rebelled. They sacked three towns, Camulodunum (Colchester), Verulamium (St Albans) and Londinium (London), slaying 70,000 Romans and their allies.

A strong Roman army quickly crushed the rebellion and Boudica poisoned herself.

◀WHO WERE KNOWN AS THE BARBARIANS?

A number of Germanic tribes living in northern and central Europe were called barbarians. They included the Alamanni, Franks, Goths, Heruli and Vandals.

The ancient Greeks coined the name 'barbarian' to describe all foreigners who did not speak Greek. They thought that the strangers' unintelligible languages sounded like 'Bar . . . bar . . .'

From this it was only a step to use the term barbarian to describe apparently less cultured peoples. The Greeks and the Romans did this.

The northern frontier of the Roman Empire lay on a line marked by two rivers, the Rhine and the Danube. This frontier was 2,400 km long, and even a Roman army of 400,000 was not enough to defend it against barbarian attacks.

The barbarians finally conquered the Western Roman Empire in AD 476. The Eastern or Byzantine Empire lasted until 1453, when it fell to the Ottoman Turks.

▶WHO WERE JUSTINIAN AND THEODORA?

Justinian was the most brilliant ruler of the Byzantine, or Eastern Roman, Empire. He was married to Theodora.

Justinian was born Flavius Petrus Sabbatius near Skopje in present-day Yugoslavia in AD 483. He took the name Justinian after his uncle the Emperor Justin I, whom he succeeded in 527.

Theodora was said to be the beautiful daughter of a circus bearkeeper. Justinian married her in 523.

Theodora had great influence over her husband and over the empire. But although she was brave, she was not strong and died at about the age of 40 in 548.

Justinian built up his weakened empire. His most important work was to collect together all Roman law into the *Corpus Juris Civilis* which forms the basis of continental European law today. His restless energy earned him the nickname 'the emperor who never sleeps'. He died in 565.

▶WHO WAS MUHAMMAD?

Muhammad was the founder of the Islamic religion. Its followers, the Muslims, call him the Prophet of God.

The prophet was born in Mecca, now in Saudi Arabia, in about AD 570. An orphan, he was brought up by his uncle to be a shepherd and camel driver.

In 595 Muhammad married a rich widow, Khadija, who was 15 years older than he. For many years he led a peaceful life as a merchant in Mecca. When he was about 40 he had a vision of the Archangel Gabriel, calling him to preach the word of God. He began preaching in 613.

In 620 Khadija died. By this time Muhammad had made many enemies and he was forced to flee. He took refuge at the oasis of Yathrib, now Medina, city of the prophet.

By 630 Muhammad had established his new religion and by the time he died in 632 he was chief of all Arabia. His teachings were recorded in the Koran, the sacred book of Islam, as revelations from God.

◀WHO WAS HARUN AL-RASCHID?

Harun al-Raschid was the Caliph (ruler) of Baghdad, now the capital of Iraq. He ruled from 786 to 809.

Under Harun's rule Baghdad became the centre of the Arab world. Harun's empire covered south-western Asia and northern Africa.

The Caliph had diplomatic relations with the T'ang emperors of China and with the Emperor Charlemagne in France. He was engaged in wars with the Byzantine (East Roman) Empire from 791 to his death.

Baghdad was a very rich city and nowhere was richer than Harun's own court. It was full of musicians, poets, singing girls and jesters, as well as scholars and religious leaders.

A fictional account of Harun's court is contained in the *Thousand and One Nights*, a collection of love stories and fairy tales. But Harun was not the hero that these stories make out. At times he could be cruel.

◄WHO WAS CHARLEMAGNE?

Charlemagne was king of the Franks (French) from 771 to 814. He made himself Emperor of the West in an attempt to revive the Roman Empire.

Charlemagne means 'Charles the Great'. His lands included France and parts of what are now Belgium, the Netherlands, Germany and Austria. Later he added Corsica, most of Italy, a strip of northern Spain and, after a long war, Saxony to his empire.

On Christmas Day 800 Pope Leo III crowned Charles as Emperor of the West.

Charlemagne was a great admirer of learning, encouraged literature and the arts at the Frankish court and founded a school at Aachen, his capital. Its director was an English monk, Alcuin of York. The emperor himself studied there. His handwriting was bad, from which grew a legend that he could not write. In fact he wrote a hymn, *Veni, Creator Spiritus*.

▼WHO FOUGHT AT THE BATTLE OF TOURS?

The Battle of Tours was fought in 732. A Frankish army under Charles Martel crushed a Moorish invasion.

The Moors, Muslims from North Africa, occupied most of Spain in 711. In 732 the Moorish ruler of Córdoba, Abd-ah-Rahman, led an army of 80,000 men hoping to conquer Gaul (France).

The Moors swept through southern France, killing and looting. They reached as far north as Tours, where Charles and his army turned them back.

Although the battle is usually called Tours, it was actually fought at Poitiers, about 100 km further south. Abd-ah-Rahman died in the fight, and his followers fled. This ended the last major attempt by the Moors to conquer Europe.

Charles acquired his surname Martel (the Hammer) because of his victory.

►WHO WAS FREDERICK BARBAROSSA?

Frederick I was the first German ruler to adopt the title Holy Roman Emperor. He was nicknamed Barbarossa because of his red beard.

Frederick inherited the title Duke of Swabia from his father. The throne of Germany came from his uncle, Conrad III, in 1152.

Having made his position in Germany secure, Frederick spent the next 30 years trying to conquer Italy. Finally he gave up and granted the Italian states their independence.

In 1187 the Saracens (Muslims) captured Jerusalem. Christians in Europe rushed to mount the Third Crusade to win the Holy Land from Islam. Frederick at once took over as leader and organized an expedition.

He set out in 1189 at the head of a large army. The year after, he was drowned leading his men across the River Saleph in Cilicia (now in Turkey). Many legends have grown up around this hero-king.

▶WHO WAS WILLIAM THE CONQUEROR?

William was Duke of Normandy, in France. In 1066 he conquered England. He was a harsh ruler but a brilliant statesman.

Robert the Devil, Duke of Normandy, had no legitimate heir so he nominated William, his illegitimate son, to succeed him. William was only a boy when Robert died, but he soon asserted his strong will.

By the time he was 27 he had crushed several revolts in Normandy and defeated his overlord, Henry I of France, who tried to take Normandy.

William had a slight claim to the English throne. It is said that he was promised it by the Saxon king, Edward the Confessor, who had no heir, but when Edward died the English chose a Saxon earl, Harold Godwinesson, as king. So William invaded England and defeated and killed Harold at the Battle of Hastings.

William was firm and ruthless, but he brought peace and a stable government to the land he had conquered.

◀WHO WAS ELEANOR OF AQUITAINE?

Eleanor was a French princess who inherited the vast Duchy of Aquitaine from her father. She married Louis VII of France, then Henry II of England, and played a vital role in both French and English political and cultural life.

Eleanor married Louis in 1137 when she was about 15 years old. They had two daughters. Louis then became very pious and Eleanor claimed he was 'more like a monk than a king'.

The pope annulled the marriage in 1152, and two months later Eleanor married the energetic, red-haired Henry, Count of Anjou, 11 years her junior, but a man much more to her taste. She became a great patroness of poets and musicians.

In 1153 Henry became king of England. His marriage gave him half of France as well as England, so making him one of the most powerful monarchs in Europe.

▶WHO WERE AVICENNA AND AVERROËS?

These two men were both Arabic physicians and philosophers whose work had a great influence on European philosophers and thinkers.

Avicenna (left) lived from 980 to 1037, spending much of his life in Persia. His real name, in Arabic, was abu-Ali al-Husain ibn-Sina. His philosophy was based on that of the Greek scholar Aristotle.

He wrote about 100 books. His most famous one was an encyclopedia of medicine. It was studied not only in the Arab world but – in translation – by European doctors as late as the 1500s.

Averroës was a Spanish Arab who lived from 1126 to 1198. His name in Arabic was abu-al-Walid Muhammad ibn-Ahmad ibn-Rushd. He was born at Córdoba in Spain where he became chief judge. He wrote books on astronomy, grammar, law and medicine.

◀ WHO WAS SALADIN?

Saladin was the greatest Saracen (Muslim) general at the time of the Third Crusade. He was sultan of Syria and Egypt.

Saladin was born in 1138, the son of Ayyub, governor of Damascus. His name in Arabic was Salah al-Din Yusuf ibn-Ayyub. After years of campaigning to protect Egypt from the Christians he became Sultan in 1174.

Saladin, a devoted Muslim, resolved to drive the Christians from Palestine, where they had set up kingdoms after the First and Second Crusades. In 1187 he launched a drive through Palestine, capturing Jerusalem.

When news of his victory reached western Europe the Third Crusade was proclaimed. It was led by Richard I (the Lion-Heart) of England and Philip II of France. After three years' fighting Richard and Saladin made a truce.

Saladin died soon after. He was renowned for his courage, military skill, and chivalry.

▶ WHO WAS FRANCIS OF ASSISI?

Francis founded three religious orders whose members are called Franciscans. Many people regard him as a saint.

The real name of Francis was Giovanni Francesco Bernardone. He was born at Assisi in central Italy in 1182. His father was a wealthy merchant.

Francis was a carefree young man of the world until service in war, captivity and the sight of extreme poverty changed him. One day he thought he heard a voice saying 'Francis, repair my falling house'.

He quarrelled with his father, gave up all his worldly goods and, dressed only in a hair shirt and a cloak, went off to live a life of poverty.

Soon he gathered some like-minded men around him and founded the order of Friars Minor. Later orders were the Poor Clares, for women, and the Tertiaries, for lay people as well as monks and nuns. He was famous for his love of birds and other animals.

▲ WHO WAS TAMERLANE?

Timur Lenk – Tamerlane, or Timur the Lame – was a Mongol chief who conquered an empire stretching from India to Turkey.

Timur was the son of a Mongol chief whose tribe lived near Samarkand, now in the Soviet Union. He became a mercenary soldier in Afghanistan. During this period he was wounded in the leg and so acquired his nickname.

By 1370, when he was 34, Timur had built up an army with which he conquered Samarkand and a large area around it. From there he began a series of 35 campaigns. His first conquests were Persia, Afghanistan, Azerbaijan and Kurdistan.

He then marched north into Russia. After this he invaded India and sacked Delhi. He died in 1405 while marching to attack China with 200,000 men.

◀WHO WERE FERDINAND AND ISABELLA?

Ferdinand inherited the kingdom of Aragon; Isabella became queen of Castile. Their marriage united most of Spain.

When Ferdinand was born in 1452 Spain consisted of the poor Christian kingdoms of Aragon, Castile and Navarre, and the Moorish (Arab) province of Granada.

Ferdinand married Isabella in 1469. Isabella inherited her kingdom in 1474 and Ferdinand became king of Aragon in 1479.

The couple were fanatical Christians. They started an Inquisition to suppress heresy and harass the Jews. In 1492 their armies drove the Moors from Granada.

The same year they agreed to finance an Italian sailor, Christopher Columbus, to sail under the Spanish flag to find a westward route to the Indies. He discovered America.

So this royal marriage led to the unification of Spain, the discovery of America and the creation of a Spanish empire.

▶WHO WAS LEONARDO DA VINCI?

Leonardo was one of the world's most talented people. He was a painter, sculptor, architect, anatomist, scientist, inventor, engineer and musician.

This extraordinary man was born at Vinci, in Italy, in 1452 and died in France in 1519. He was a leading figure of the Renaissance, the rebirth of learning which lasted from the 1400s to about 1600.

He worked for Lorenzo the Magnificent in Florence, Lodovico Sforza in Milan, Cesare Borgia in Romagna and Francis I in France.

Leonardo began many projects, but finished only a few. His artistic masterpiece is the wall painting of the Last Supper at the Monastery of Santa Maria delle Grazie, Milan.

He is noted for his advanced knowledge of anatomy.

The volumes of notebooks and drawings that he left show that he wrote not only left handed but also in 'mirror writing', possibly so that people would not steal his ideas.

◀WHO WAS LORENZO THE MAGNIFICENT?

Lorenzo was a member of the powerful Medici family which dominated Florence and Tuscany in Italy from the mid-1300s to the 1600s.

At the age of 20 Lorenzo succeeded his father who died in 1469. At that time the city-state of Florence was a republic. Like his father and grandfather Lorenzo had no formal title, apart from *magnifico signore*, magnificent lord.

Lorenzo ruled with the aid of a council but was in fact a dictator. His skill in diplomacy helped to keep Florence strong and his ability to manipulate finances helped to make Florence prosperous.

Il magnifico is best remembered as a patron of the arts – not so much for the glory of his city as for his own private collection. His writings helped to make the Italian spoken in Tuscany the national language of all Italy.

▶WHO WAS KNOWN AS IL MORO?

Il Moro, the Moor, was the nickname given to Lodovico Sforza, Duke of Milan, because of his dark hair and his swarthy complexion.

Lodovico, born in 1451, was the younger brother of Galeazzo Maria Sforza, Duke of Milan. Galeazzo was vain and cruel. In 1476 three of his subjects killed him. He was succeeded by his seven-year-old son, Giangaleazzo, with Lodovico as regent.

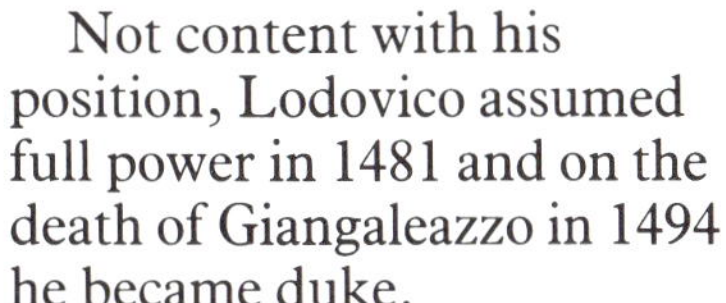

Not content with his position, Lodovico assumed full power in 1481 and on the death of Giangaleazzo in 1494 he became duke.

However, he feared that Giangaleazzo's friends would rebel against him, so he invited the French to enter Italy and help him.

This move proved his undoing. The French turned on him and drove him from power. Though he was restored to his dukedom by the Swiss, they too turned on him. From 1500 to his death in 1508 he was a prisoner of the French.

◀WHO WAS ERASMUS?

Desiderius Erasmus was a Dutch scholar and writer who tried to reform the Roman Catholic Church from within.

Erasmus was made a priest in 1492 but rebelled against the monastic lifestyle. Having studied in Paris for a while, he became a wandering scholar in the early 1500s, dividing his time between England, France, Italy and the Netherlands.

Erasmus campaigned for reform through his mildly humorous writing satirizing the many corrupt practices that were harming the work of the Church.

Most of his work aimed at trying to make theology more accurate and he reformed the text of the New Testament. But he got caught in the middle of quarrels between Protestants and Catholics.

Before he died in 1536 in Switzerland, Erasmus saw the Reformation in full flood, with Protestants breaking from Rome. But Erasmus was a moderate and this was not the kind of reformation that he had intended.

▶WHO WAS CALVIN?

John Calvin was a French theologian, one of the leaders of the Reformation.

Calvin's name was originally Jean Chauvin. In later years he used a Latin version of the name, Calvinus.

He was born at Noyon, in Picardy, in 1509. His father originally wanted him to study theology and become a priest but later persuaded him to become a lawyer instead.

Calvin was converted to Protestantism about 1534 and was exiled from France. He went to Geneva, where he and other Protestants tried to set up a religious government.

The Genevese revolted against this idea, so Calvin retired to teach theology in Strasbourg. However, there was chaos and anarchy in Geneva and he was asked to come back in 1541.

In Geneva Calvin set up a very strict religious and civic government, for a time even abolishing taverns and the use of non-Biblical Christian names. His Protestantism became known as Calvinism.

▲WHO MET AT THE COUNCIL OF TRENT?

The Council of Trent was a series of conferences at which bishops of the Roman Catholic Church met between 1545 and 1563 at Trento, in northern Italy.

The purpose of the council was to redefine various beliefs of the Church and to reform some bad practices that had grown up.

It was a major move in the Counter-Reformation, the Roman Catholic Church's answer to Protestantism.

The council was called by Pope Paul III. He hoped that representatives of the Protestant Churches would attend but only a few did so – and they would not accept the authority of the council.

The first session, which lasted from 1545 to 1547, was attended by 72 bishops and their advisers. The second, in 1551-52, attracted only 59.

The final session, from 1561 to 1563, was attended by 235 Church leaders including six cardinals, as well as eight ambassadors. The council's decrees were agreed by Pope Pius IV in 1564.

▼WHO WAS SULEIMAN THE MAGNIFICENT?

Suleiman I was one of the most important sultans of the Ottoman Turkish empire. He ruled from 1520 to 1566.

'The Magnificent' was the title by which Suleiman was known to Europeans, but to his own people he was 'The Lawgiver' because of reforms in law and government which were carried out during his reign.

The magnificent side of Suleiman's character was shown in his drive to extend his empire. He added to it in turn Belgrade, Budapest, Rhodes, Tabriz, Baghdad, Aden and Algiers, with the territories around them.

His major campaigns were against Persia. During one campaign he besieged Vienna.

Suleiman was infatuated by a beautiful Russian slave, Roxalana, whom he took to be his concubine. To please her he had his legitimate sons, Bayazid and Mustafa, put to death so that Roxalana's son, Selim, could succeed him as the next sultan. Sulieman died in 1566 while besieging a fortress in Hungary.

▼WHO WERE THE JANISSARIES?

The janissaries were a picked body of soldiers who formed the core of the Ottoman Turkish army.

The name janissary comes from the Turkish *yeni çeri*, which means 'new soldiery'. The corps was formed sometime in the 1400s as the first regular Ottoman army.

The earliest janissaries were recruited from children of Christian people under Turkish rule. These children were carefully selected and taken from their parents to be brought up as Muslims.

However, the recruitment of Christian children had stopped by 1700, when the janissaries were merely a corps of picked men, including many Turks.

Although the janissaries were expected to provide their own weapons, they proved to be a formidable fighting force. Their numbers rose from 12,000 to more than 500,000.

The janissaries rebelled several times, deposing sultans and supporting new ones. In 1826 Sultan Mahmud II abolished the corps.

▼WHO WERE THE HABSBURGS?

The Habsburgs were a German royal family who ruled in Europe for more than 600 years.

The family took its name from *Habichtsburg* (Hawk's Castle) a fortress built at Aargau near Zürich in Switzerland in 1020.

Count Rudolf IV of Habsburg was elected as Holy Roman Emperor (ruler of the German lands) in 1273, with the title Rudolf I. From then until 1806, when the empire came to an end, most of its rulers were Habsburgs.

The most powerful Habsburg was the Emperor Charles V, who was elected in 1519. He was already King of Spain, Duke of Burgundy and ruler of the Spanish Netherlands (modern Belgium and the Netherlands), Sicily, Naples, Sardinia and the West Indies.

Other lands Charles inherited or acquired later included Austria, Bohemia, Hungary, Peru and Mexico.

By 1556 Charles had had enough. He abdicated and retired to a monastery in Spain, dying in 1558.

▼WHO WAS QUEEN ELIZABETH I?

Elizabeth was the last Tudor ruler of England. Under her inspired leadership England became a wealthy and powerful nation.

Elizabeth was the daughter of Henry VIII and his second wife, Anne Boleyn. She was brought up to be a fine scholar.

She succeeded her elder sister, Mary I, in 1588. Mary had tried to restore Roman Catholicism in England. Elizabeth led the country back to Protestantism.

She was a skilled diplomat and never married because of the problems that marriage might bring.

England was a rival of Spain for the riches of the New World. Elizabeth kept the two countries from going to war for as long as she could, but when Philip I of Spain sent a large fleet, the Armada, to invade England she personally urged her sailors on to victory.

Poetry, music and drama flourished during her reign, which encouraged talented men like William Shakespeare.

▲WHO WAS THE FIRST BOURBON KING OF FRANCE?

Henry III, king of Navarre, became king of France as Henry IV in 1589. He succeeded his brother-in-law, Henry III of France, who was assassinated.

Henry of Navarre was descended from Louis IX, king of France in 1226-70. His ancestors held the title Duke of Bourbon. He inherited the French throne when the Valois family had no more heirs after Henry III.

Henry IV was leader of the Huguenots, the French Protestants. He adopted the Roman Catholic faith to please the majority of his subjects, observing cynically, 'Paris is worth a Mass'.

Civil war had been raging in France between Huguenots and Catholics. Henry helped to stop the fighting by the Edict of Nantes, which gave the Huguenots equal political rights.

Henry paid off France's debts, and set up a strong army. He was murdered in 1610 by a mad schoolmaster, François Ravaillac.

◀WHO IS KNOWN AS THE FATHER OF MODERN PHILOSOPHY?

Philosophy today is based largely on the work of the French mathematician, scientist and philosopher René Descartes.

Descartes was born in 1596. He had a private income so he was able to devote most of his life to studying and writing.

He believed that it is possible to arrive at the truth by reason alone. His starting point was the Latin phrase *Cogito, ergo sum* 'I think, therefore I am'.

He used this theory to prove that humans are real, that if a person is thinking he must be alive to be doing so. He went on by logical steps to prove that the world and God exist.

Descartes's writings made him many admirers. In 1649 he was invited to visit Queen Christina of Sweden. She wanted him to teach her philosophy. But the bitter cold of a Swedish winter gave him pneumonia from which he died in 1650, aged 53.

▶WHICH CARDINAL MADE THE KINGS OF FRANCE SUPREME?

The cardinal was Armand Jean du Plessis, duke of Richelieu, who served as chief minister of Louis XIII from 1624 to 1642.

Richelieu became bishop of Luzon in 1606, when he was 21 – the post was given to his family as a reward for military services. He was made cardinal in 1622 and duke in 1631.

Richelieu ruled France well. He began by curbing the power of the nobles. He then ended the political privileges of the Huguenots, the French Protestants. His actions made the king, acting through his chief minister, the supreme power in France.

In foreign affairs Richelieu determined to curb the power of the Habsburgs, the ruling family in Germany. Although he was a leader of the Roman Catholic Church, he took France into alliance with the Protestant enemies of the Catholic Habsburg emperor.

He founded the French Academy in 1635.

◀WHO BECAME THE LORD PROTECTOR OF ENGLAND?

The title of Lord Protector was given to Oliver Cromwell in 1653, after the English Civil War.

Cromwell was born in 1599. He was a country gentleman, farming his estates, until he was 41.

In 1640 he was elected a member of Parliament. He took part in the quarrel between Parliament and King Charles I and when war broke out between king and Parliament, Cromwell raised a troop of cavalry. His soldiers were known as 'Ironsides'. He was inspired by his deeply-held Puritan faith.

After taking a leading part in the trial and execution of Charles, Cromwell tried to make Parliament efficient, but failed. His supporters in the army then dissolved Parliament and made Cromwell Lord Protector – he refused the title of king.

Though he called two Parliaments Cromwell ruled as a dictator until his death in 1658.

▶ WHO WAS CATHERINE THE GREAT?

Catherine II was Empress of Russia for 34 years, from 1762 to 1796.

Catherine was a German princess. Her original name was Sophia Augusta Frederica of Anhalt-Zerbst. She was married to the Emperor Peter III of Russia.

Catherine was 16 in 1745 when she married. She was witty and well educated; Peter was weak in body and mind. At that time he was heir to his aunt, the Empress Elizabeth.

Six months after Peter became emperor, Catherine and some army officers deposed him. He died a few weeks later.

Catherine proved to be a good ruler, especially in foreign affairs. Russia acquired the Crimea from the Turks.

At home Catherine improved medical care, education (for women especially) and religious toleration. But she extended serfdom, a form of slavery.

Catherine worked long hours on government business and on her books and plays.

◀ WHO WAS MARIE ANTOINETTE?

Marie Antoinette was an Austrian princess who became queen consort of Louis XVI of France. She was executed during the French Revolution.

The marriage of Louis, then heir to the throne, and Marie Antoinette, an attractive, intelligent girl of 15, took place in 1770. It was arranged to cement an alliance between Austria and France.

Louis was slow thinking and slow moving. His wife was quick, vivacious and energetic. For these reasons Marie Antoinette played a large part in affairs of state at a time when France was in turmoil.

At that time the rich in France were very rich and the poor very poor. Through ignorance Marie Antoinette just did not understand the plight of the poor, who thought that she was extravagant. People mistrusted her because she was Austrian.

In 1793 the revolutionaries tried her for treason, and she was sent to the guillotine.

▶ WHO WAS FREDERICK THE GREAT?

Frederick II, known as The Great, was King of Prussia, a German country now divided between Russia, Poland and East Germany.

Frederick became king in 1740 when he was 28. He had been trained as a soldier but had spent a lot of his time studying music and philosophy.

Almost at once he became involved in the War of the Austrian Succession, in which several rival claimants tried to take the throne of Austria from Empress Maria Theresa.

Frederick's main motive in the war was to seize the province of Silesia from Austria, which he did. He proved to be a brilliant general.

In the course of later wars he acquired territory from Poland. But the cost of war weakened the economy which he had to build up again during the last years of his reign.

As Frederick was a good flute player he attracted to his court many fine musicians.

▼WHO WAS JEAN JACQUES ROUSSEAU?

Rousseau was a French philosopher, writer and musician. His liberal thinking helped to influence the people who started the French Revolution.

Rousseau was born in Geneva, in Switzerland, the son of a watchmaker. His early years were spent wandering, doing a variety of jobs, none of them for long. By turns he was in a notary's office, an apprentice engraver, a servant, a secretary and a music teacher.

In 1742 he settled in Paris where he wrote operas and ballets and earned small sums by copying music. He also contributed articles on music to the *Encyclopédie*, the first major French encyclopedia.

Rousseau won fame in 1750 with a *Discourse on the Sciences and the Arts*, an essay in which he claimed arts and sciences had corrupted mankind.

His later writings, especially *The Social Contract* (1762), influenced political thought, while his *Confessions* (1770) set a fashion in candid autobiography.

▲WHO WROTE *THE RIGHTS OF MAN*?

The author of *The Rights of Man* was Thomas Paine, an English-born political writer and agitator.

Thomas Paine was the son of a Quaker corsetmaker. His early life was unsuccessful; in 1774 he was sacked from his job as a tax man and left for America.

There his pamphlet *Common Sense*, urging the colonists to break with Britain, helped to influence many people towards declaring independence.

Paine returned to Europe in 1787. In England he wrote *The Rights of Man* (1791-92), a treatise in which he justified the French Revolution, then raging.

The treatise outraged the British government. Paine was tried for treason and outlawed. He went to France where he became a French citizen and a member of the National Convention.

But Paine's views soon made him enemies in France. He was imprisoned. In 1802 he was allowed to return to America where he died in poverty in 1809.

▲WHO DRAFTED THE AMERICAN DECLARATION OF INDEPENDENCE?

The first draft of the Declaration was made by Thomas Jefferson, a delegate to the Continental Congress of the 13 American Colonies in 1776.

Jefferson did his work so well that the full Congress made few changes in the final Declaration.

He was a remarkable man. He was born in 1743 in a well-to-do Virginia family, married an heiress and became a busy lawyer. He was well read, collected books and played the violin.

He began his political career in the Virginia assembly, then became State governor. In 1783 he was elected to the Federal Congress, and devised America's decimal currency.

Jefferson then followed Benjamin Franklin as US Ambassador to France and four years later became Secretary of State. After that he was elected vice-president (1797-1801) and president (1801-1809). As president, he bought Louisiana from France.

▲WHO WERE THE JACOBINS AND GIRONDINS?

Jacobins and Girondins were the members of the two main political groups during the French Revolution, from 1789 to 1794.

The Jacobins were members of the Jacobin Club which took its name from the Rue St Jacques, the Paris address of its headquarters.

The Girondins, who were less extreme than the Jacobins, got their name from the Gironde, the home of many of their leaders, in southwestern France.

The Girondins' main leaders were Maximin Isnard, Jacques Pierre Brissot and Jean Marie Roland and his wife. They believed in private ownership of property and wanted to set up a federal republic.

The Jacobins, led by Maximilien Robespierre, gained power in 1793, sending many Girondins to the guillotine in the Reign of Terror. The next year Robespierre himself was executed, the Jacobins lost power and the Reign of Terror came to an end.

▲WHO WAS MADAME ROLAND?

Madame Roland was the wife of an author and scientist who was one of the leaders of the French Revolution.

Madame Roland was born Jeanne Manon Phlipon. She married Jean Marie Roland de la Platière in 1780. The couple were enthusiastic supporters of the 1789 revolution.

The revolutionaries split into two major groups, the Jacobins and the Girondins. The Rolands were members of the Girondins.

Madame Roland, charming, witty and patriotic, was the centre of the group. In 1793 the Jacobins, who had the upper hand, arrested many Girondin leaders, including Madame Roland. After a travesty of a trial she was condemned to die.

An old friend, Henriette Cannet, wanted to change places with her.

Madame Roland gently refused. When the time came she went to the guillotine calmly, saying 'O Liberty, what crimes are committed in thy name!'

▼WHO WAS THE FIRST PRESIDENT OF THE UNITED STATES?

The first president was George Washington, who had led the American armies in the War of Independence. He served from 1789 to 1797.

Washington was born in Virginia in 1732. After working as a surveyor he became a soldier, joining the Virginia Militia at 21.

At the age of 26 he retired to spend the next 14 years as a gentleman-farmer. He also served in the Virginia Legislature.

When war came between Britain and its 13 American colonies, Washington was unanimously chosen as the American commander-in-chief. Through eight years of hardship Washington and his army, seldom more than 10,000 men, won a series of battles and campaigns.

After five years of retirement Washington helped draw up the US constitution. He was then elected president, but by the time his second term ended he was glad to retire again. He died in 1799.

◀WHO WAS GARIBALDI?

Giuseppe Garibaldi was one of three patriots who worked to unite Italy and free it from foreign rule.

Garibaldi was born in 1807. He took part in an unsuccessful rebellion in Piedmont in 1834. He fled to South America where he spent the years 1836-48 in guerrilla warfare.

In 1848 he fought in an army trying to defend the newly-formed Roman republic against French and Austrian attacks. After it was defeated he settled in America.

He returned to Italy in 1854. By this time Count Camillo Cavour, premier of Piedmont, and Giuseppe Mazzini, whose patriotism had originally inspired Garibaldi, were working to start a new revolt.

In 1860 Garibaldi led a force of 1089 volunteers, the Redshirts, in a landing on Sicily, which he freed from its Spanish Bourbon rulers. He then conquered the mainland part of the Sicilian kingdom which led to the uniting of Italy. He failed to free Rome, then under the Pope's rule.

◀WHO WAS THE FIRST KING OF A UNITED ITALY?

The king was Victor Emmanuel II, ruler of Piedmont-Sardinia. He was the only non-clerical Italian to rule any part of Italy.

In the early 1800s Italy was divided into seven states. One, the Papal States, was ruled by the Pope. The Kingdom of the Two Sicilies – Sicily and southern Italy – was ruled by a Spanish Bourbon king. The rest was under Austrian control.

In most of these states political opponents of their governments were arrested, tortured and imprisoned.

A series of secret societies was formed to fight foreign domination. Among the main conspirators were Giuseppe Mazzini, and Giuseppe Garibaldi.

Political freedom and unity for Italy were eventually gained largely through the prime minister of Piedmont-Sardinia, Count Camillo Cavour. By uniting revolt with diplomacy, he placed Victor Emmanuel on the throne of a united Italy by 1861.

▶WHO WAS 'THE WIDOW AT WINDSOR'?

The widow was Queen Victoria, the British monarch who had the longest reign. She was a widow for 40 years.

Victoria was 18 when she became queen in succession to her uncle, William IV, in 1837. In 1840 she married her first cousin, Prince Albert of Saxe-Coburg-Gotha.

Albert died of typhoid fever in 1861, leaving Victoria desolate. She mourned for much of the rest of her reign.

Victoria and Albert had nine children. At her death Victoria had about 37 great-grandchildren and was related to almost all the royal families of Europe.

Five of her granddaughters married monarchs – the Tsar of Russia and the kings of Greece, Norway, Romania and Spain. A grandson became Kaiser (emperor) of Germany. A great-granddaughter married the king of Sweden.

The kings of Hanover and the Belgians were Victoria's uncles. One cousin married the queen of Portugal, another the Emperor Maximilian of Brazil.

▶ WHO WAS KNOWN AS THE IRON CHANCELLOR?

The 'Iron Chancellor' was Otto von Bismarck, the Prussian statesman who united Germany in 1871.

Bismarck was born in 1815. He was a *Junker*, a country squire. He studied law, became a member of the Prussian Diet (parliament) and served as ambassador to Russia and France. In 1862 he was appointed prime minister.

Bismarck led Prussia into three successful wars: in 1864 it defeated Denmark, in 1866 Austria and in 1871 France. Bismarck is generally thought to have provoked France into declaring war in order to unite the German states.

After France's defeat Bismarck persuaded the German princes to offer the crown to the Prussian king, William I, who became the first *Kaiser* (emperor) of Germany.

William created Bismarck a prince and Chancellor of the new Germany. He was known as the 'Iron Chancellor' because he said problems should be solved by 'blood and iron'.

▶ WHO WAS ABRAHAM LINCOLN?

Abraham Lincoln was the 16th president of the United States. He kept the country together during the civil war of 1861-65.

Lincoln was a farmer's son. He worked in a village store, then as a surveyor and as a postmaster. Meanwhile he studied to become a lawyer.

He served first in the Illinois legislature (State Parliament) and then as a Congressman. He became an opponent of slavery. He did not want to abolish it but he did not want it to spread either, particularly in the new territories of Kansas and Nebraska.

In 1860 Lincoln was elected president. Knowing his views on slavery, seven Southern states broke away from the Union. Four more followed.

This led to civil war. Lincoln worked hard for victory over the rebel states and to ensure their return to the Union. Five days after the fighting ended in April 1865 Lincoln was shot dead at a theatre.

◀ WHO WAS THE EMPRESS-DOWAGER?

The Empress-Dowager was Tz'u-hsi of China who lived from 1835 to 1908 and ruled for many years.

Tz'u-hsi was a wife of the Emperor Hsien-feng and mother of Emperor T'ung-chih. She was regent for her son who died in 1875.

He was followed on the throne by his cousin, Ch'ing Kuang-hsu, then aged three. Tz'u-hsi, still in control of China, remained so until 1889.

Because the Empress-Dowager disliked change she fought against any attempts to modernize China. But when the Emperor assumed power he listened to the advice of reformers. In a series of decrees he announced changes in schooling, the civil service, the armed forces and the construction of railways.

Horrified, Tz'u-hsi seized power again. She had the young emperor imprisoned and stopped all reforms. It was in vain: three years after her death China became a republic.

◀WHO FORMED THE FIRST TRADE UNIONS?

The earliest trade unions were probably the trade clubs formed by workers in various trades, such as carpenters and shoemakers, in the 1600s.

Associations of workers in a number of trades existed from medieval times. But the early groups were guilds of craftsmen rather than unions of less skilled workers.

Before the 1700s people tended to work at home or in very small groups.

Trade unions as we know them today grew up when men, women and children worked in factories created during the Industrial Revolution.

In Europe most governments passed laws in the late 1700s which banned associations of workers. In the United States unions were not made illegal, but they made little progress.

Modern trade unions, for unskilled and semi-skilled workers as well as craftsmen, grew up during the second half of the 19th century.

◀WHO WERE THE SUFFRAGETTES?

The name 'suffragettes' was given to women who took militant action in support of women's suffrage – that is, the right to vote.

Campaigns for women's suffrage began in many countries during the 1800s. Campaigning in the United States began in earnest in 1848, and by 1869 Wyoming had given women the right to vote. In 1920 the US gave all women the vote.

At the start of campaigning in Britain in 1865 it met with stiff opposition. But militancy did not begin until 1905 when two women rose to ask questions about the vote at a Liberal Party meeting and were ejected brutally.

Thereafter the suffragettes damaged property in Britain, went to prison, and while in prison went on hunger strike. Some women over 30 received the vote in 1918 and all women over 21 did so in 1928.

France and Italy did not grant women's suffrage until after World War II.

◀WHO CREATED THE RED ARMY?

The Red Army was the army of the Bolshevik (Communist) government which took power in Russia in 1917. It was organized by Leon Trotsky.

Trotsky, born in 1879, was one of the Bolshevik leaders who seized power. His original name was Lev Davidovich Bronstein but he took a new name as a revolutionary leader.

Trotsky was second only in importance to Vladimir Lenin, the head of the Bolshevik government.

The Red Army was formed in January 1918. It consisted at first only of volunteer workers and peasants but it lacked good officers. Trotsky recruited officers of the old tsarist army.

Soon afterwards a number of anti-Communist groups tried to set up rival governments. These, called Whites, were crushed by the Red Army.

After Lenin's death Trotsky was sent into exile. Lenin's successor, Joseph Stalin, had Trotsky assassinated in Mexico City in 1940.

▶ WHO FOUNDED THE SOVIET UNION?

The founder of the Soviet Union – more correctly, the Union of Soviet Socialist Republics – was Vladimir Lenin.

Lenin was born Vladimir Ilyich Ulyanov in 1870 but he later took the name Lenin.

Lenin opposed the monarchy in Russia after his elder brother was executed for plotting to kill the tsar. His Communist views caused him to be exiled to Siberia in 1895. When he was released in 1900 he left Russia and began plotting revolution.

The revolution began in March 1917 while Lenin was still abroad. He hurried home, won the support of many soldiers, sailors and workers, and overthrew the new Liberal-Democratic government of Russia in November 1917.

By 1921 Lenin had eliminated all opposition and had made Russia the Communist state it is today. He retired after a stroke in 1922 and died in 1924.

▶ WHO WAS KNOWN AS THE MAHATMA?

Mahatma, which is a Sanskrit word meaning 'great soul', was the term of affection applied by Indians to Mohandas Karamchand Gandhi, who worked to free his land from British rule.

Gandhi was born in 1869. He studied law in London then went to South Africa to work. There he led many campaigns on behalf of Indians who were suffering from discrimination.

He devised a system of non-violent civil disobedience which he called *satyagraha*.

Gandhi returned to India in 1915. He was a small, frail man who wore traditional Indian dress and lived simply and frugally. In spite of his weak appearance he led a long campaign for Indian independence which was finally achieved in 1947.

He tried to stop the feud between Hindus and Muslims, but he was assassinated in 1948 by one of his own Hindu people who disliked Gandhi's tolerance of all religions.

▶ WHO FOUNDED MODERN TURKEY?

The Republic of Turkey was founded by the general and statesman Kemal Atatürk.

His name was originally Mustafa. While at the army staff college in Istanbul his skill in mathematics earned him the name 'Kemal', which means perfection.

When Mustafa Kemal was born in 1881, Turkey, then called the Ottoman Empire, was ruled by a sultan. During World War I it sided with Germany and was defeated.

After the war, in which he had risen to the rank of general, Kemal organized a nationalist movement to resist foreign control. The nationalists then overthrew the sultan and proclaimed a republic, with Kemal as its president.

Kemal modernized his country, liberating women, improving education and introducing the Western alphabet instead of Arabic. In 1934 he took the surname Atatürk, Father of Turks. He died in 1938.

▶ WHO WAS BENITO MUSSOLINI?

Mussolini was a Fascist who ruled Italy as a dictator from 1922 to 1943. He was known as Il Duce (The Leader).

Mussolini was born in 1883. He was first a teacher, then a journalist and political agitator.

In 1919 he founded the Fascist Party, named after the axe-like symbol of power in ancient Rome. The party was strongly nationalistic and opposed to Communism.

The Fascists used armed gangs, the Blackshirts, to attack the opposition, especially all Left-wing organizations. They became so powerful that in 1922 Mussolini was asked to form a government.

To increase Italy's power he conquered Ethiopia in 1935-36. In 1939 he seized Albania. His closest ally was the German dictator Adolf Hitler, who led Italy unwillingly into World War II. After Italy was heavily defeated, Mussolini was overthrown and shot.

▶ WHO WAS STALIN?

Joseph Stalin was dictator of the Union of Soviet Socialist Republics. He led Russia to victory in World War II but had millions of Russians 'liquidated'.

Stalin lived from 1879 to 1953. His name was Iosif Dzhugashvili, but he took the name Stalin, meaning 'steel', in 1913.

After the Revolution Stalin became secretary of the Communist Party. When Lenin died in 1924 Stalin made himself leader.

In a series of five-year plans Stalin's government reorganized farming and industry and did away with private businesses. People lived in fear of the secret police. Any potential opponents were killed in a series of purges in 1935-37.

In 1939 Stalin signed a pact with Hitler, agreeing to carve up Poland and not to go to war. But two years later Hitler invaded Russia. At the end of the war Stalin set up Communist rule in six eastern European countries.

◀ WHO WAS TITO?

Tito led Yugoslavia's resistance to the Germans in World War II and became his country's Communist president.

Tito was born in 1892, a peasant's son, named Josip Broz. He fought in the Austrian army in World War I until he was captured by the Russians. In Russia he became a Communist.

In 1920 he returned to his homeland, Croatia, now part of the new country of Yugoslavia, and there organized a Communist party.

During the war, Tito – a name he adopted in 1934 – led a group of Communist resistance fighters known as the Partisans.

Unlike the other eastern Europe Communist countries, Yugoslavia under Tito stayed independent of Moscow, despite all threats.

Both during the war and after, Tito proved he was a born organizer, capable of taking the right decisions in difficult circumstances. He died in 1980.

▼WHO WAS ADOLF HITLER?

Hitler ruled Germany as a dictator from 1933 to 1945. He started World War II.

Hitler was born in Austria in 1889. He wanted to be an artist but was not talented enough. In World War I he was decorated for bravery.

After the war he formed the National Socialist Party, 'Nazis' for short. In 1933 he was made chancellor (prime minister).

Within six months Hitler had eliminated all rival political parties, and soon after had his rivals among the Nazis put to death. Hitler was master of Germany, known as *Der Führer* (The Leader).

Hitler began persecuting the Jews, rearmed Germany and set out to conquer Europe. In turn he seized Austria, Czechoslovakia and most of Western Europe. It took the combined forces of Britain, Russia and the United States to crush him. He committed suicide in 1945.

◀WHO WAS WINSTON CHURCHILL?

Churchill was a soldier, statesman and writer who became Britain's leader during World War II.

Churchill's full name was Winston Leonard Spencer-Churchill. He was the grandson of the seventh Duke of Marlborough.

He began his career as a soldier and by the time he was 24 he had taken part in three campaigns and written a book.

In 1901 Churchill was elected a Conservative MP. Three years later he changed parties to become a Liberal. During World War I and after he held many high posts in government, served as a soldier again for a time and became a Conservative again.

From 1929 to 1939 Churchill was out of office but with the start of World War II he was back in government. From 1940 to 1945, when he was Prime Minister, his speeches and courage inspired the country. He held the office again from 1951 to 1955. He died in 1965.

▶WHO WAS MAO ZEDONG?

Mao Zedong – Mao Tse-tung in the older form of his name – ruled China for 27 years.

In 1921 revolutionary leader Mao helped to found the Chinese Communist Party. In 1928 the Nationalists who ruled China launched an attack on Jiangxi province where the Communists had their base.

In 1934 Mao led his Communist 'Red Army' to safety in Shaanxi province, in what is called the Long March.

In 1937 the Communists and their rivals formed an alliance against the Japanese who had invaded China. But they fell out again in 1946. By 1949 the Communists had won and Mao ruled China.

He quickly organized his people towards modernizing the country. He achieved cultural and economic changes that surprised the world – the 'Great Leap Forward' of 1958 and the 'Cultural Revolution' of 1966.

From 1959 to his death in 1976 Mao was chairman of the Communist party.

◀WHO UNIFIED SAUDI ARABIA?

Arabia was conquered and unified by Ibn Saud who lived from about 1880 to 1953.

The family of Saud ruled a large part of Arabia in the early 1800s, but by 1891 the family was in exile in Kuwait. Some of Arabia belonged to the Ottoman (Turkish) empire and the rest was small kingdoms.

In 1902 a young Saudi leader, 'Abd al-'Aziz ibn 'Abd al-Rahman ibn Faisal al Sa'ud, began the reconquest of his family's former lands. With 200 men he seized Riyadh, the present capital, and the territory around it.

In 1913 Ibn Saud, as he became known, seized the Persian Gulf coastline between Qatar and Kuwait from the Turks. By 1922 he ruled the whole of central Arabia, the Nedj, and took the title Sultan of Nedj.

In 1926 Ibn Saud conquered Hejaz (the Red Sea coast) and in 1932 he proclaimed his lands to be one kingdom under the name of Saudi Arabia. Money from oil made it rich.

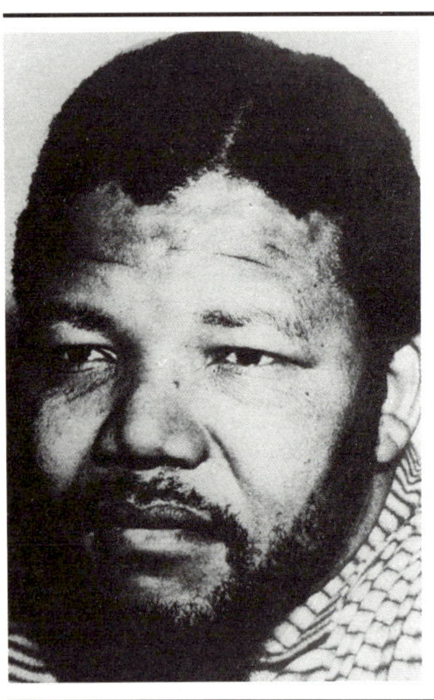

◀WHO FORMED THE AFRICAN NATIONAL CONGRESS?

The African National Congress was formed by a group of African leaders in 1912 at a conference held at Bloemfontein, South Africa.

The leaders were tribal chiefs, lawyers, clergymen and businessmen from all over South Africa, who were trying to improve the status of Black Africans in South Africa.

The congress made little progress until the 1940s, when the Reverend James Calata, then secretary-general, reorganized it into a strong nationalist party.

In 1952 a campaign of passive resistance to apartheid (racial segregation) laws was launched. More than 8,000 Africans were jailed. One of its leaders, Chief Albert Luthuli, was awarded the 1960 Nobel Peace Prize.

In 1960 the South African government banned the African National Congress but **Nelson Mandela (left) led** it until he was jailed for life on terrorism charges in 1963.

◀WHO WAS HO CHI MINH?

Ho Chi Minh founded the Communist state of North Vietnam which he ruled until his death in 1969.

Ho was born in 1890 and named Nguyen That Thanh. He took the name Ho Chi Minh, which means 'He Who Shines', in 1941.

Ho went to Europe in 1911 and while there helped to found the French Communist party.

Indochina was occupied by the Japanese during World War II. In 1945, with Chinese backing, Ho entered Vietnam and proclaimed a Communist republic. From 1946 to 1954 Ho's troops fought the French. Vietnam was divided in two, with the north under Ho's Communist rule.

In 1957 Communist guerrillas, the Viet Cong, began fighting against the repressive government of South Vietnam. Ho backed them, and a full-scale war ensued with the United States supporting the south. Ho died before the war ended in a Communist victory.

▶ WHO WAS MARTIN LUTHER KING?

King was a Black Baptist minister and civil rights leader who tried to gain equal rights for Blacks. He was killed in 1968.

Martin Luther King, Jr. was the son of a Baptist minister. He began his equal rights campaign in 1955 when he led a boycott of buses in his home town, Montgomery, Alabama because the bus company made Blacks occupy rear seats.

The campaign succeeded. King always emphasized non-violence and racial brotherhood, but he was subjected to violence himself: bombs were thrown at his home, he was stoned in Chicago and stabbed in New York City. But he carried on and was awarded the 1964 Nobel Peace Prize.

In 1967 King spent five days in jail for demonstrating.

For 1968 King planned a 'Poor People's March', but before it could take place a white ex-convict gunned him down at a strike in Memphis, Tennessee.

▶ WHO ARE THE PALESTINIANS?

Palestinians are people of Palestine, the historic land now covered by Israel, the West Bank part of Jordan and the Gaza Strip, and especially Arab refugees from this region.

The United Nations divided Palestine in 1947 into two countries, one for Jews and one for Arabs. Before partition took place in May 1948 Arabs and Jews fought fiercely, and a stream of Arab refugees began to pour out of Palestine.

The flood of refugees grew following two massacres in April 1948, one of Arabs by Jews, one of Jews by Arabs.

Neighbouring Arab countries tried to destroy the new Jewish state, Israel, in May 1948 but failed. Meanwhile the number of refugees rose to 700,000. Many set up camps in the Gaza Strip.

The Palestine Liberation Organization (PLO) was set up in 1964 to fight for Arab rights in Palestine. The number of Palestinian refugees had risen to over 2,000,000 by 1984.

▶ WHICH RELIGION DO SUNNIS AND SHI-ITES BELONG TO?

Sunnis and Shi-ites form the principal divisions of Islam. The groups split in the AD 600s.

The Sunni Muslims are the main body of Islam. They are followers of *sunna* (the way) of the Prophet Muhammad. About nine-tenths of the world's 513,000,000 Muslims are Sunnis.

The Shi-ites broke away from the larger group of Muslims over a question of leadership. In 656 Ali became caliph (ruler) of the Arab empire. He was a cousin of Muhammad who had married the Prophet's daughter.

But several Muslims, including Mu'awiya the governor of Syria, refused to accept Ali as caliph. There was some warfare, which lasted until Ali was assassinated by another sect, the Kharijites.

Ali's supporters were called the Shi'at Ali, the party of Ali. From being a political group they became a separate religious sect. Their main support is in Iran and Iraq.

SCIENCE AND TECHNOLOGY

▼WHO DISCOVERED MAGNETISM?

The first person to find out about magnetism is believed to have been Thales. He was a scientist who lived in Greece about 2500 years ago. He discovered that a mineral called lodestone attracts pieces of iron. This is because lodestone is magnetic.

Thales was born in about 624 BC and lived until about 546 BC. He was the first great scientist known. Thales not only discovered magnetism but also electricity. He rubbed pieces of amber and found that light objects would stick to them. This is because the amber is given a charge of static electricity. The Greek word for amber is *electron* and this is the origin of the word electricity.

▶WHO WAS PYTHAGORAS?

Pythagoras lived in Greece from about 560 BC to about 500 BC. He founded one of the greatest Greek schools of philosophy, in southern Italy, which lasted on and off for 800 years. He and his followers believed that they could use numbers to explain everything. This idea led them to make important discoveries in mathematics and in music.

Pythagoras and his followers developed a theory of numbers. They believed that everything can be explained by finding a simple relation between the numbers involved. In music, they found that the notes played by strings or pipes sound pleasing to the ear if the lengths of the pipes or strings are in simple proportions to each other – for example, if one pipe or string is half, three-quarters or two-thirds the length of another.

The theory of numbers led Pythagoras and his followers to develop basic ideas in astronomy and mathematics. They believed that the Earth is round and that it moves in an orbit like the other planets because the sizes of the orbits of the planets would be in simple proportions.

Pythagoras also discovered a theory in geometry that is named after him. It explains that in a right-angled triangle the length of the hypotenuse (side opposite the right-angle) squared, is equal to the squares of the other two sides added together.

▶ WHO FIRST THOUGHT OF ATOMS?

Everything is made of atoms. Atoms are very tiny particles. They are so small that they can be seen only in the most powerful microscopes. Leucippos, who was born in Greece in about 490 BC, first thought of atoms. His ideas were true, but few people believed him. Atoms were not actually discovered until less than 200 years ago.

We know of Leucippos from the writings of his pupil Democritos. They believed that if you could cut something into smaller and smaller pieces, you would eventually get down to particles that you could not divide further. They called these particles 'atoms' (which means 'uncuttable' in Greek) and reasoned correctly that atoms must exist because this explains why objects are different – they are made of different kinds of atoms linked together.

◀ WHO WAS THE FATHER OF GEOMETRY?

Geometry is a branch of mathematics. It deals with shapes like triangles and squares and their sizes. Euclid, a Greek philosopher who was born in about 330 BC, wrote the first book on geometry and he is known as the father of geometry.

Euclid's book, *Elements*, contains proofs of many theories in geometry, including that of Pythagoras. A proof explains why a theory is correct, and Euclid's proofs were so clever that they are still used today.

Little is known about Euclid's life, but according to a later Greek philosopher he founded the first school of mathematics in Alexandria.

Euclid taught geometry to King Ptolemy of Egypt, who complained of having to learn Euclid's proofs. Euclid replied, 'There is no royal road to geometry'.

▶ WHO MADE A FAMOUS DISCOVERY IN HIS BATH?

In about 250 BC, the Greek scientist Archimedes was asked by King Hieron to find out if his crown was pure gold. Archimedes thought and thought about the problem. Suddenly, the answer came to him when he was having a bath.

As he got into the bath, Archimedes realized that if he immersed the king's crown in a vessel full to the brim with water, it would cause some water to overflow. If he then immersed a piece of pure gold of the same weight as the crown, the same amount of water would overflow if the crown was pure gold. In this way, Archimedes found that the crown was not pure gold.

He is believed to have rushed naked from his bath into the street shouting 'Eureka', which means 'I've found it'.

Archimedes made many important scientific discoveries, including pulleys, and he first explained why things float.

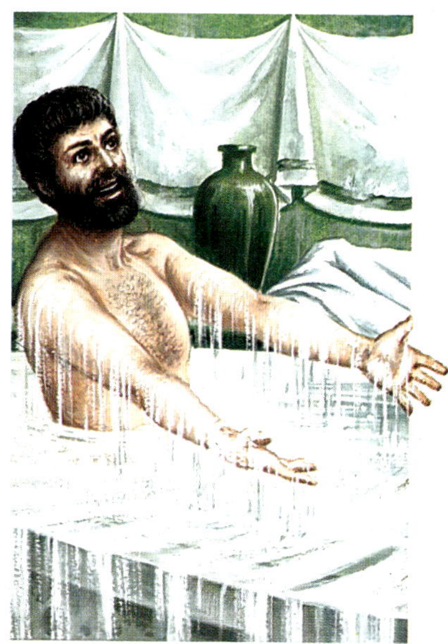

◀WHO INVENTED THE SEISMOGRAPH?

A seismograph is an instrument that detects earthquakes. The first one was made in China in about AD 100 by Chang Heng.

The seismograph was about 2 metres across and had eight dragon heads around the top, each holding a ball. If an earthquake happened, the instrument shook. A ball dropped from the mouth of one of the dragons into the mouth of the toad below.

The ball that fell indicated the direction of the centre of the earthquake. Inside, a heavy weight hung from the top of the instrument. When the seismograph shook, the weight swung. Levers connected the weight to the dragon heads and one of them tilted to open the mouth of a dragon head so that the ball was released. The other dragon heads locked so that only one ball fell.

The seismograph was used to find where an earthquake had occurred so that help could be sent there.

▶WHO WAS HERO OF ALEXANDRIA?

Hero of Alexandria was a Greek inventor who lived at Alexandria in Egypt. He was born in about AD 20. Hero's most famous invention was a steam engine. Steam made by boiling water in a vessel was piped to a sphere. The steam spurted out of two jets on the sphere and made it turn. The engine was in Hero's time treated like a toy. Using steam for power was not realized until the 1700s when steam engines were rediscovered and revolutionised the world of transport and technology.

Hero's steam engine worked because the steam spurting out of each jet forced the sphere to move in the opposite direction, causing the sphere to turn in the same way as the water jets on a lawn sprinkler make it spin. The jet engines on aircraft work on the same principle as Hero's engine.

Hero made many other inventions, using devices such as gears, levers and mirrors. They included a kind of taxi meter for chariots. Gears attached to the wheel of the chariot caused a pointer to move as the chariot travelled over the ground, indicating the distance that the chariot had gone. However, many of Hero's inventions had no practical use and were mostly mechanical toys. He made a model theatre, for example, in which figures of actors moved about automatically, and a temple in which the doors opened when a fire burned on the altar. Hero's purpose may not only have been to entertain people but also to demonstrate the principles on which levers, mirrors and other devices work.

Hero was also the first person to understand the nature of air. He explained that air can be compressed into a smaller space, reasoning correctly that air is made of atoms that move closer together as the air is compressed. Hero also discovered the principles by which mirrors reflect light rays.

▶WHO WAS THE FIRST MODERN SCIENTIST?

Many people consider that the first modern scientist was Galileo, who lived in Italy from 1564 to 1642. The important scientific discoveries made in ancient Greece were lost during the Dark Ages and Middle Ages. After they were rediscovered, Galileo was the first great scientist to advance science and make new discoveries.

Galileo was the first person to use a telescope in astronomy and he made several important discoveries, including the moons of Jupiter. He also found out how objects move when they fall. He did this by timing the movement of balls rolling down a slope. By conducting experiments and using measurement to prove that his ideas were correct, Galileo laid down the principles of the experimental method that modern scientists use to make discoveries.

◀WHO INVENTED THE BAROMETER?

A barometer measures the pressure of air. The Italian scientist Evangelista Torricelli invented the barometer in 1643. He found that the pressure of the air forces mercury up a tube to a certain height. This height is a measure of the air pressure.

Torricelli filled a long glass tube with mercury, then placed it upside-down in a dish of mercury. The pressure of the air pushing down upon the surface of the mercury in the dish supported the column of mercury in the tube. Torricelli noticed that the height of the column varied from day to day. He realized that this was because the air pressure changed slightly. By measuring the height of the mercury column, he was able to measure the pressure of the air. A vacuum existed in the tube above the mercury, the first vacuum ever produced.

◀WHO INVENTED THE PENDULUM CLOCK?

A pendulum clock has a swinging pendulum that makes the clock keep time. The first working pendulum clock was made by Christiaan Huygens in Holland in 1657. It was the first accurate clock.

A pendulum always takes exactly the same time to swing to and fro. The pendulum was discovered by Galileo in about 1583 when he watched a lamp swinging in Pisa cathedral. He realized that if the hands of a clock were connected to a pendulum, they could be made to move slightly every time the pendulum swung. By having a pendulum of the right length, the hands would move at the right rate to measure the time. However, Galileo was unable to make a successful pendulum clock. A complicated mechanism was needed, which Huygens invented after studying pendulums.

▼WHO INVENTED THE MICROSCOPE?

No single person invented the kind of microscope we use today, which has two or more lenses. It was developed by several scientists in Holland, Italy and Britain from about 1600 onwards.

The first compound microscopes, which contain two or more lenses, appeared in the 1600s. They did not give a very sharp image. The first scientist to make important observations with a microscope was Anton von Leeuwenhoek, who lived in Holland from 1632 to 1723. He used home-made single-lens microscopes. These were tiny but very powerful magnifying glasses which could magnify objects several hundred times. The microscopes gave a very sharp image and Leeuwenhoek made several great discoveries using them. He observed the single-celled animals called protozoa and he was also the first person to observe bacteria.

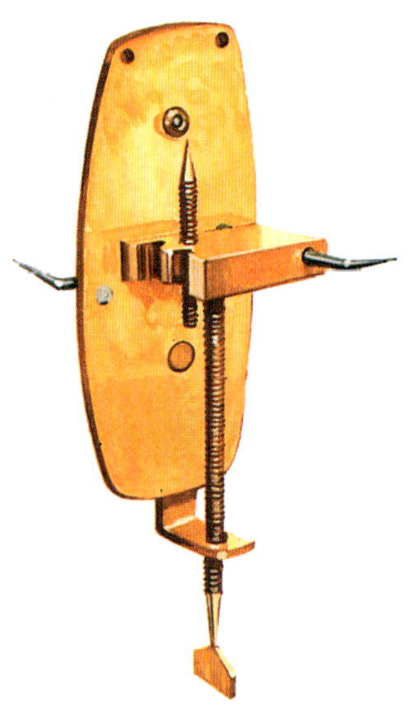

▲WHO FIRST USED A MICROSCOPE TO OBSERVE LIVING TISSUE?

Marcello Malpighi, who lived in Italy from 1628 to 1694, first examined living tissue through a microscope. By observing frogs' lungs, Malpighi saw how oxygen from the air is dissolved in the blood.

He was the first to describe the structure of the brain and spinal cord and gave the first accurate description of blood and muscle cells as well as many other features of human anatomy.

He also examined the wings of a bat and found that they contain tiny blood channels called capillaries. This discovery was very important because it explained how blood circulates around the body. The capillaries connect the arteries to the veins so that blood can flow back to the heart.

Another important discovery was made with the microscope by the Dutch biologist Jan Swammerdam. He first observed the red cells of the blood in 1658.

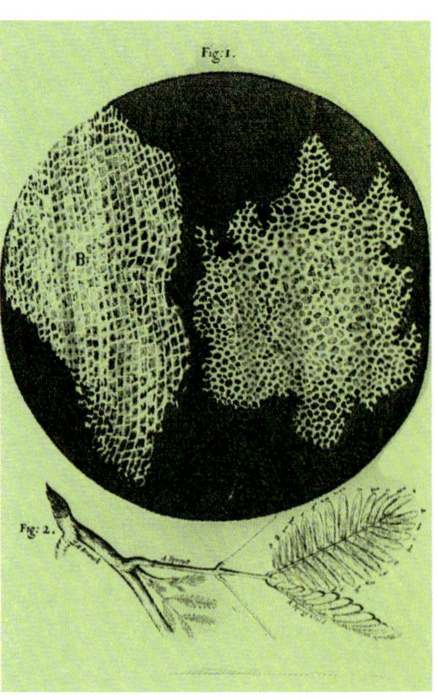

▲WHO DISCOVERED CELLS?

All living things are made up of cells. The cells are usually very small and can be seen only in a microscope. The first scientists to use microscopes observed cells but did not realize what they were. The British scientist Robert Hooke gave cells their name when he observed them in cork.

Robert Hooke wrote the first important book on microscopes. It was called *Micrographia* and was published in 1665. It contains superb drawings of the many objects and living things Hooke observed with his microscope. Among them were the tiny holes which can be seen in cork from the bark of a cork-oak tree. A slice of cork appeared to be made of hollow compartments which Hooke called cells. Hooke made several other important discoveries in physics.

◀WHO DISCOVERED WHY RAINBOWS HAPPEN?

People realized long ago that rainbows form when rain is lit up by the Sun. The raindrops change the sunlight into colours. Isaac Newton proved this by putting a glass prism in a beam of sunlight. It produced a rainbow pattern of colours, showing that white light is a mixture of colours. Raindrops act like tiny prisms to form a rainbow.

Newton showed without doubt that white light is a mixture of colours by using another prism. He placed it in the beam of colours produced by the first prism and obtained a beam of white light. The second prism combined the colours to give white light. Newton did this experiment in 1665 or 1666. He went on to invent the reflecting telescope, which uses a curved mirror instead of a lens, in 1668. The large telescopes used by astronomers are reflecting telescopes.

▲WHO DISCOVERED GRAVITY?

Things fall to the ground because a force called gravity pulls them down. The first person to realize this was the British scientist Isaac Newton, who lived from 1642 to 1727. Newton said that he made this discovery when he saw an apple fall to the ground.

Newton observed the apple in 1665. He wondered if the Earth has a force of gravity which would also act on the Moon and keep the Moon in orbit around the Earth. Newton then made some calculations to prove his theory that there is a law of gravity obeyed by everything in the Universe. His results did not support his theory, possibly because he did not have the correct figure for the size of the Earth. It was not until about 20 years later that Newton was finally able to prove his law, which is known as the universal law of gravitation.

▶WHO INVENTED THE AIR PUMP?

The first person to pump the air out of a container was Otto von Guericke. He lived in Germany from 1602 to 1686. Guericke invented the air pump in 1647. At that time, many people thought that a vacuum could not exist. Guericke made the air pump to produce a vacuum.

Guericke made spectacular demonstrations using his air pump. He put a clock inside a glass jar and showed that its sound disappeared as the air was removed. This was because sound cannot travel through a vacuum. He also showed that a burning candle goes out if the air is removed from it. In 1657, he astounded people by placing two hemispheres together and pumping out the air inside. He then hitched two teams of horses to the hemispheres to pull them apart. The horses failed because the outside pressure of the air acting on the hemispheres was too strong for them.

◀WHO FLEW A KITE IN A THUNDERSTORM?

In 1752, the American scientist Benjamin Franklin carried out one of the most dangerous experiments ever performed. He flew a kite in a thunderstorm in order to show that lightning is a form of electricity. Others who tried this experiment were killed by lightning.

Franklin flew his kite into thunderclouds in order to show that they contain high charges of electricity. He proved this by producing sparks from the end of the string of the kite. By doing this experiment, Franklin understood how lightning strikes and he went on to invent the lightning conductor. Franklin was also the first person to realize that an electric charge is either positive or negative.

Benjamin Franklin was also a great statesman. He played a very important part in the founding of the United States of America.

▶WHO FIRST FOUND OUT WHAT PREHISTORIC ANIMALS WERE LIKE?

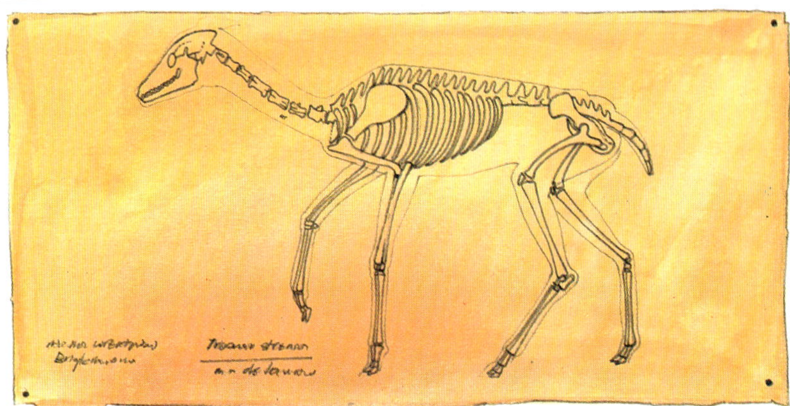

The first person to study prehistoric animals was the French scientist Georges Cuvier. He looked at the bones in the fossil remains of an animal and worked out how they fitted together. From this, he was able to describe the appearance of the live animal.

Cuvier's first success was in 1796, when he discovered a prehistoric elephant different from any living kind of elephant. His greatest achievement was to identify a prehistoric flying reptile, which he called a pterodactyl. Cuvier was followed by the British zoologist Richard Owen, who discovered dinosaurs and built the first full-scale replicas in 1854.

▶WHO FIRST CLASSIFIED PLANTS AND ANIMALS?

All plants and animals have Latin or scientific names as well as common names. The common names are different in different places. But the Latin name of a plant or animal does not change, so anyone can identify a plant or animal from its Latin name. Carolus Linnaeus invented this system of classifying living things in 1735.

Linnaeus developed his classification system by placing plants or animals in different groups. If two or more plants or animals were similar in particular ways, they were placed in the same group. If two or more groups were alike, they were put in a larger group and so on. The Latin or scientific name therefore indicates to which groups a plant or animal belongs. This indicates the possible relationships between different animals and how similar ones may have evolved from a common ancestor.

▶ WHO FIRST CALCULATED THE AGE OF THE EARTH?

People have long tried to work out the age of the Earth. In the 1600s, an Irish archbishop decided from reading scriptures that the world was created in 4004 BC. But geologists later realized by examining rocks that it is much older.

The person who founded the science of geology was James Hutton (right), who lived in Britain from 1726 to 1797. He travelled widely to study the shape of the land and the rocks in different places.

Hutton concluded that the land changed shape very slowly, and that its features had taken a very long time to form. From his work, Charles Lyell later estimated that rocks must be hundreds of millions of years old. We now know by studying meteorites that the Earth formed about 4500 million years ago.

◀ WHO FIRST PRODUCED AN ELECTRIC CURRENT?

Luigi Galvani, an Italian doctor, first produced an electric current in the 1780s. He hung some frogs' legs on iron railings with copper hooks. He noticed that the legs twitched. The reason was that the metals produced a weak electric current in them.

The moisture in the frogs' legs connected the different metals in the hooks and railings, causing an electric current to be produced in the same way as a battery. The electric current then made the muscles contract, causing the legs to twitch. This explanation was put forward by Volta, who later invented the battery. Galvani never believed it. He was convinced that animals contain electricity and that electricity came from the frogs' legs.

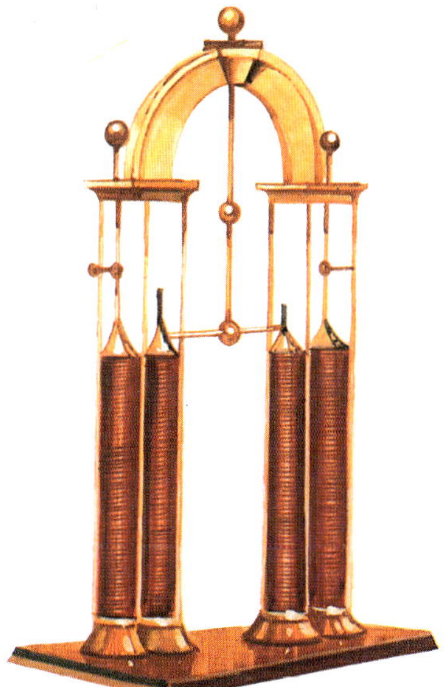

◀ WHO INVENTED THE BATTERY?

The battery was invented by the Italian scientist Alessandro Volta in 1800. It was made of a pile of silver and zinc discs with layers of cardboard soaked in salty water between them. The 'voltaic pile', as it was called, produced a strong electric current.

Volta got the idea for the battery from the work of Galvani. He realized that placing pairs of different metals in contact with solutions of salt and other substances would cause an electric current to flow. He then investigated different metals and solutions to find out which gave the most current. Placing several pairs of discs on top of each other to form the voltaic pile increased the current in the same way as connecting several batteries together with wire.

In honour of his discovery, the electric unit called the volt is named after Volta.

◀WHO FIRST PROVED THAT ATOMS EXIST?

Philosophers in ancient Greece first thought of atoms. But they could not prove that all things are actually made of atoms. In 1803, the British scientist John Dalton was able to prove that this is true, even though atoms were too small to be seen with the microscopes made at that time.

Dalton knew that all substances are made of elements. Water is made of hydrogen and oxygen, for example. Also, any amount of a pure substance always contains the same elements in the same proportions. Dalton showed that this is because atoms of the elements are linked in these proportions in a pure substance. In water, there are always two hydrogen atoms for every oxygen atom. Dalton also showed that atoms of different elements have different weights.

▶WHO WAS CHARLES DARWIN?

Charles Darwin was a British scientist who lived from 1809 to 1882. He first showed that all living things evolve. This happens because when an animal is born, it may be very slightly different from its parents. Thus over many generations, the animal may change its form and slowly evolve into a different kind of animal. This is called evolution. Darwin's theory of evolution was published in 1859.

Darwin got much of his evidence for evolution during a five-year voyage around the world. He saw many different kinds of animals and came to believe that one kind of animal evolves into another. But he could not explain why this should happen. After the voyage, Darwin spent more than 20 years working out how evolution occurs. His theory suggested that evolution is the result of natural selection. This means that new kinds of animals evolve because they are better fitted to survive in their surroundings than other kinds, which may gradually die out.

His theory also showed why there are many different kinds of animals in the world. They have evolved from other kinds of animals in the past. Different kinds of plants have evolved too and also human beings, probably from ape-like creatures.

One important piece of evidence was the group of finches that Darwin discovered on the Galapagos Islands in South America. These birds are alike but have different kinds of beaks. Darwin suggested that all had evolved from one kind of finch that flew to the islands in the past. As they bred and spread over the islands, the finches found new kinds of food, and they evolved into several different kinds of finches adapted to eat the different foods available to them. Some now eat seeds, some cones or nuts and others feed on insects.

▶ WHO DISCOVERED THE LAWS OF HEREDITY?

Heredity makes children resemble both their parents in certain ways. Animals and plants pass on their features too. The person who discovered how heredity works was a monk called Gregor Mendel. He lived in Czechoslovakia from 1822 to 1884. Mendel discovered the laws of heredity by planting peas in his monastery's garden and studying the plants that grew.

Mendel was a monk who devoted years of study to heredity. He grew many generations of peas, crossing one kind with another to see which features were passed on to the next generation.

He found that the kinds of peas which grew depended on the combinations of features in the parent plants. He was then able to produce laws that explain how heredity works. However, Mendel was ignored and his laws were not believed until about 50 years later.

◀ WHO LINKED ELECTRICITY AND MAGNETISM?

The Danish scientist Hans Oersted discovered that electricity produces magnetism in 1820. He placed a compass needle near a wire. When an electric current flowed in the wire, the needle moved because the current made the wire magnetic.

Oersted's discovery of a link between electricity and magnetism was very important. Soon afterwards, the British scientist Michael Faraday used it to make the first electric motor. Electricity fed to the motor produces a magnetic field that makes magnets turn inside the motor. Faraday later invented the electric generator, in which electricity is made by turning coils of wire in a magnetic field. Transformers change electricity into magnetism and back again.

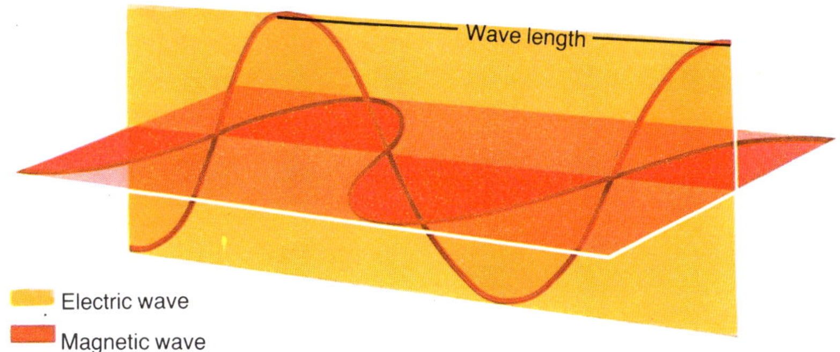

▲ WHO DISCOVERED THE NATURE OF LIGHT?

Light is made of electricity and magnetism. This was discovered by the British scientist James Clerk Maxwell. It took him nearly 20 years to work out the nature of light. He succeeded in 1873.

Maxwell was fascinated by light. Twelve years earlier, he made the first colour photograph, which was of a tartan ribbon.

Maxwell knew that electricity and magnetism were linked, and worked out that if rays consisting of electric and magnetic fields could exist, they would travel at the speed of light. He therefore suggested that light is an electromagnetic radiation. If so, Maxwell said that other kinds of electromagnetic radiation must also exist. Another kind – radio – was discovered in 1888, after Maxwell's death.

◀ WHO CLASSIFIED THE ELEMENTS?

There are just over a hundred elements of which everything is made. They fall into several groups of elements that are alike. The first person to realize this was the Russian scientist Dmitri Mendeleyev. In 1869, he published a table of the elements showing them in their groups.

Mendeleyev's table is still used to classify the elements. When Mendeleyev published it, 63 elements were known. Mendeleyev placed similar elements in the same groups in the table but gaps resulted. Instead of changing the table to remove the gaps, Mendeleyev said that the gaps represented elements that had not been discovered. From their position in the table, he predicted what three of these elements would be. All three were discovered shortly after and they were exactly as Mendeleyev had forecast.

▶ WHO MADE MORE THAN 1000 INVENTIONS?

Thomas Edison made almost 1300 inventions in his lifetime. Edison lived in the United States from 1847 to 1931. His most famous invention was the phonograph in 1877. The phonograph recorded sound in the same way as the gramophone but the records were cylinders instead of flat discs. Edison made the very first recording, which was of himself reciting 'Mary had a little lamb'.

Edison did not make all his inventions single-handed. After several early successes, he set up a team of scientists to work for him. This was the first research laboratory, and Edison directed investigations into any field that might produce a useful invention.

In addition to sound recording, Edison made or contributed to several other important inventions. He invented an electric light bulb in 1879. However, the British scientist Joseph Swan also invented one at the same time, so both men share the credit for it. The telephone was invented by Alexander Graham Bell in 1876, but Edison quickly improved it into a practical instrument that people could use. In 1881, Edison built a power station to supply electricity to homes. This and another power station in Britain were the world's first power stations.

Edison was one of several inventors who developed motion pictures. His research team had the idea of placing the pictures on a strip of film and the first public film show took place at Edison's laboratories in 1891. Edison's contribution to radio was to discover the Edison effect, which causes an electric current to flow through a vacuum in an electronic valve or tube. The effect was discovered in 1883 and later used by others to make valves for the first radio sets. The Edison effect is also used in the picture tube of a television set.

▲WHO DISCOVERED RADIOACTIVITY?

Radioactivity consists of invisible rays. They were discovered in 1896 by the French scientist Antoine Becquerel. He detected the rays coming from a mineral containing uranium, which is now used as a nuclear fuel. Radioactivity is also called radiation and it can be harmful. The radiation sign above is used to warn people of radioactivity.

Becquerel discovered radioactivity by accident. He placed a piece of uranium mineral on a photographic plate, which was wrapped in black paper so that it would not be exposed to the light. Luckily, Becquerel did not use the plate but decided to develop it. He found that it was strongly fogged as if light had got to it. Becquerel realized that invisible rays from the mineral had penetrated the paper and caused the plate to fog. Marie Curie later named this radioactivity.

▲WHO REVOLUTIONIZED PHYSICS IN 1900?

Physics is the branch of science that studies energy. In 1900, the German scientist Max Planck produced a new theory called the quantum theory. Before that time, scientists could not understand several effects of energy. Because the quantum theory could answer many important questions on energy, it totally changed physics.

The quantum theory explained that energy in the form of light and other rays or waves is made up of minute particles of energy. A particle of energy is called a 'quantum' of energy. A quantum of light is also known as a 'photon'. Using this theory, scientists were later able to explain how atoms can receive and produce energy. The quantum theory also explains how electricity is produced from light in photoelectric or solar cells.

▲WHO DISCOVERED RADIUM?

Marie Curie, who was born in Poland but lived in France, discovered radium with her husband Pierre Curie. They thought that a mineral called pitchblende contained an unknown element. It took them four years to produce the element, because the mineral had a very small amount of it. They called the new element radium, and it is used to treat the dangerous illness cancer.

Pitchblende is radioactive and the Curies thought that this was due to radium. They had to treat eight tons of pitchblende to get just one gram of radium. The extraction process did not remove the radioactivity and the new element turned out to be very highly radioactive. This showed that radioactive rays come directly from the atoms in radioactive elements. The discovery later led to the production of nuclear energy from radioactive elements.

◀WHO FIRST SPLIT THE ATOM?

Until early in this century, scientists believed that atoms were the smallest things that could exist. Then in 1911, the British physicist Ernest Rutherford discovered that atoms are made up of even tinier particles. Six years later, Rutherford first split the atom by knocking some particles out of atoms of nitrogen gas.

Rutherford investigated atoms by firing alpha rays at them. In 1911, he found that rays were deflected by a hard particle in the centre of the atom. This was the nucleus of the atom. The nucleus turned out to contain even smaller particles called protons. Rutherford later split nitrogen atoms by firing alpha rays to knock out some protons from the nuclei. This gave oxygen atoms, the first time one element was changed into another.

▶WHO DISCOVERED RELATIVITY?

Relativity is the name of a theory that Albert Einstein first published in 1905. Einstein worked on relativity for many years and published a second theory later. Relativity is about the nature of time and space, and also mass and energy. Einstein's way of looking at these things was totally different to any that had gone before. His explanations made possible many new discoveries, one of which was nuclear power.

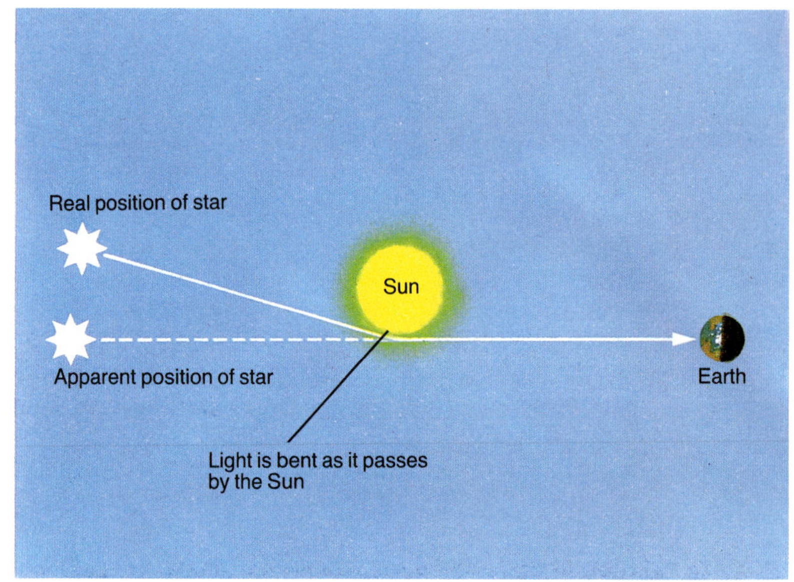

Einstein's theories of relativity produced several astonishing conclusions. One of them is that mass can be turned directly into energy, a small amount of matter giving a huge quantity of energy. This was shown to be true when nuclear energy was discovered. Another conclusion is that objects get heavier and time slows down as they move. The effect is only noticeable at extremely high speeds, and it has been observed in fast-moving nuclear particles. At the speed of light, mass would become infinite and time would stop. This means that no object (such as a spaceship) can travel at or beyond the speed of light.

Another conclusion of relativity is that the force of gravity distorts space. From this Einstein said that a strong field of gravity such as that of the Sun or a star would bend light rays, and he predicted how much bending would occur. The bending of light rays was later observed in an eclipse of the Sun, and the amount was exactly that which Einstein had forecast.

Albert Einstein was born in Germany in 1879 and lived there and in Switzerland and the United States, where he died in 1955. He is generally considered to be one of the three greatest physicists to have lived, the others being Archimedes and Isaac Newton.

▶ WHO DISCOVERED VITAMINS?

Vitamins are substances that we need for health. Illness results if any are missing from food. The need for vitamins was discovered by accident in 1896. The Dutch scientist Christiaan Eijkman found that chickens became ill if they were fed on polished rice. The reason was that polished rice lacks vitamins.

The outer covering of rice grains contains a vitamin necessary for health and polishing removes it. Eijkman did not realize this, and the discovery that we need small amounts of such substances was made by the British scientist Frederick Hopkins in 1906. He suggested that diseases such as rickets and scurvy could be cured in human beings by giving them the necessary substances. This was later found to be true and the name vitamin was given to the substances required. A number of vitamins are now known.

Vitamin A	
Thiamine B_1	
Riboflavin B_2	
Niacin	
Pyridoxine	
Pantothenic acid	
Folic acid	
Vitamin B_{12}	
Vitamin C	
Vitamin D	
Vitamin E	MANY FOODS

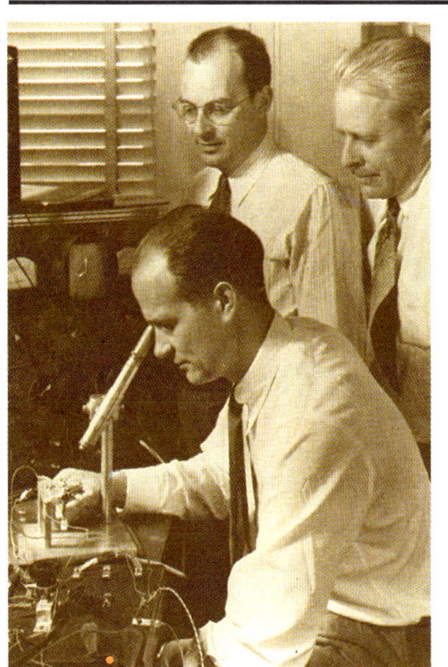

◀ WHO INVENTED THE TRANSISTOR?

Three American scientists invented the transistor in 1948. They were William Shockley, John Bardeen and Walter Brattain. Transistors replaced valves in electronic machines, being much smaller and more reliable. They made portable radio and television sets possible.

Transistors are made of pieces of silicon or other substances and amplify electric currents passing through them. Transistors can be connected together to produce small but complex electric circuits that handle signals such as those used in radio and television. In the 1950s, integrated circuits began to be made. They consist of single components containing several interconnected transistors that form a circuit. Microchips are kinds of integrated circuits containing many thousands of transistors.

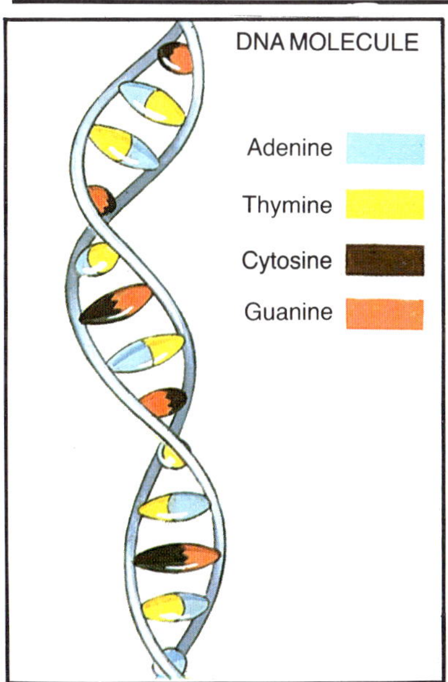

◀ WHO DISCOVERED THE STRUCTURE OF DNA?

DNA is a substance inside all the cells of living things. It governs heredity so that one generation can produce another. In 1953, the British scientist Francis Crick and the American scientist James Watson discovered the structure of DNA. This explained how heredity works.

DNA molecules in cells can make copies of themselves. In this way, new cells are produced that are exactly like the old cells. When a living thing is born, its cells are copies of its parents' cells and it inherits their features. Crick and Watson found that DNA molecules consist of groups of atoms arranged in two long intertwined strands called a double helix. The strands can form new DNA molecules in which the pattern of atoms is exactly the same. All the features of a living thing come from its DNA structure.

MYTHS, LEGENDS AND HEROES

▶WHO WERE THE AMAZONS?

The ancient Greeks told stories of a race of women warriors called Amazons. They were ruled by a queen and raised only girl children. No men or boys were allowed.

The Amazons were said to live near the Black Sea. But Greeks who settled there found no trace of them. An adventure of the Greek hero Heracles explained why. Heracles was sent to fetch the girdle of the Amazon queen Hippolyte. In doing so, the queen was killed and the Amazons were driven from their land. In revenge they fought against the Greeks during the Trojan War. But once again their queen was killed, by Achilles.

Pictures of Amazons often appear on Greek vases. In battle they wore a bow, spear, axe, shield and helmet.

The Amazon river in South America is supposed to have been named after a tribe of warrior women living there.

▶WHO HAD TO PERFORM TWELVE LABOURS?

Heracles (called Hercules by the Romans) was the most popular hero of the ancient world. Above all he was famous for his strength.

The legends of Heracles say that he was a son of the god Zeus and Alcmene. Zeus's wife Hera, who was jealous, tried to destroy the baby. She sent deadly snakes to kill him in his cradle, but Heracles was already strong enough to strangle them with his bare hands.

Hera forced Heracles to serve king Eurysthus. The king set him 12 labours, thinking them impossible for a man to perform. But Heracles completed each task.

He fought wild animals and many-headed monsters; captured man-eating horses and shot man-eating birds. He cleaned out the stables of 3000 beasts by changing the course of a river. He carried the world on his shoulders and also went into the Underworld.

Heracles had many more adventures and fought many enemies. One of these caused his death by poison. But afterwards the gods took the brave hero to live with them on Mount Olympus.

◀WHO WAS AGAMEMNON?

The legend of the Trojan War tells how for ten years a Greek army laid siege to the city of Troy. The Greek commander was Agamemnon, king of Mycenae.

Agamemnon's family lay under a curse from the gods. When his father, Atreus, was murdered, the young prince fled to Sparta with his brother Menelaus. There they married Spartan princesses.

Agamemnon later returned to Mycenae to claim his father's throne. Then he learnt that Helen, the wife of his brother Menelaus, had been stolen by Paris, son of the Trojan king. To avenge this crime, Agamemnon gathered an army from all over Greece. But to gain the gods' help he had to sacrifice his daughter Iphigenia.

The Greeks besieged Troy for ten years and finally some soldiers managed to enter the city hidden inside a wooden horse (see below). Agamemnon returned home, only to be slain by his faithless wife.

▶WHO WAS HELEN OF TROY?

The Greeks called her the most beautiful woman in the world. Her name was Helen and she was the daughter of Zeus, king of the gods. Her beauty led to the war between Greece and Troy.

Helen's mother was Leda, to whom Zeus appeared in the form of a swan. As a girl, Helen's beauty attracted the hero Theseus, who carried her off, but she was rescued by her brothers, Castor and Pollux.

Helen married King Menelaus of Sparta. Yet again, she was carried off, this time by Paris, prince of Troy. Seeking vengeance (and to recapture Helen), the Greeks sailed to war. The Greeks were victorious, Paris was killed, and Helen returned to Menelaus (although in one story she is shipwrecked in Egypt instead).

Being half goddess, Helen was believed to have divine powers. Her beauty had 'launched a thousand ships'; so she became the patron saint of Greek sailors.

◀WHICH GODDESS GAVE HER NAME TO A GREAT CITY?

The ancient Greek city of Athens grew up around a hill called the Acropolis. On it was built a temple to house the city's own guardian goddess, Athena.

Athena was a favourite child of Zeus, father of the gods of ancient Greece. She sprang fully grown and armed from her father's head – after he had swallowed her mother! The Greeks used this story to explain why Athena was goddess of both war and wisdom.

But Athena had been worshipped long before the time of the ancient Greeks. She was important to the earlier peoples of Crete and Mycenae. One Mycenaean ruler lived in a palace fort on the Acropolis. When the ancient Greeks captured it they found that he worshipped the goddess Athena. The soldiers admired the warrior goddess and adopted her as their own. They kept her sanctuary sacred and named their new city after her.

◀WHO WERE THE MUSES?

Music, art and poetry were held in high regard by the ancient Greeks. The goddesses of poetry and song were the Muses.

The nine Muses were said to be daughters of Zeus and Mnemosyne (Memory). They lived on Mount Helicon, where fresh springs gave the gift of poetry to those who drank from them. Here the Muses danced and sang.

Anyone who dared challenge the Muses in poetry or song paid dearly. When nine daughters of Pierus challenged for the prize of poetry, Apollo, the god of music, turned them into magpies!

The Muses could foretell the future and later came to represent other arts. Poetry belonged to Calliope, Erato and Terpsichore. Thalia was Comedy; Melpomene was Tragedy; and Polyhymnia was Mime. To Euterpe belonged flute-playing, while Terpsichore was also Muse of Dance. Clio was Muse of History and Urania the Muse of Astronomy.

▶WHO WAS THE QUEEN OF SHEBA?

The Bible tells of a visit made nearly 3000 years ago by the Queen of Sheba to King Solomon of Israel.

Sheba is the name the Bible gives to the country in south Arabia which today is called Yemen. In ancient times this land was rich, for it controlled the trade routes along the Red Sea to the Indian Ocean. Sheba itself was rich in gold and sweet spices, which merchants and their camel trains carried across the desert to trade.

The Queen had much to discuss with Solomon. He needed to use her trade routes to reach other lands. She needed to use his ports in Palestine to export Sheba's goods to the Mediterranean.

After the monarchs had talked and exchanged gifts, the Queen left, impressed by Solomon's wealth and wisdom.

The story of the Queen's visit is also told in the Koran, the holy book of Muslims. Arab writers call the Queen Bilqis.

◀WHO WAS APHRODITE?

Most beautiful of all the goddesses of ancient Greece was Aphrodite. As goddess of love she had power over the hearts of mortal men and women, as well as the gods.

Some stories call Aphrodite the daughter of Zeus. Others say she rose from the sea-foam near Cyprus. It may be that Aphrodite was worshipped on this island before she became known in Greece.

All stories agree about her beauty. The goddesses Hera and Athena challenged her for the title of 'the fairest' and Zeus ordered a mortal man to judge between them. The task fell to Paris, son of King Priam of Troy. All three goddesses promised a reward for his favour. Aphrodite offered Paris the most beautiful of mortal women, and won. Her gift was Helen, wife of King Menelaus.

Hera and Athena took cruel revenge by causing the Greeks to destroy Paris, his family and people in the Trojan War.

▶WHO SEARCHED FOR THE GOLDEN FLEECE?

A golden ram once flew two children across the sea. Its fleece was later hung on a tree, guarded by a dragon. To find this treasure, Jason set sail from Greece in the *Argo*.

Jason was the son of King Aeson. When Jason was a child, Pelias, Aeson's brother, seized the throne and Jason was sent away. Pelias later promised his nephew a share in the kingdom if he could bring back the Golden Fleece. Secretly he hoped to be rid of him for good.

Jason built a ship, the *Argo*, and set sail with a crew of 50 brave heroes – the Argonauts. After many strange adventures they reached Colchis, on the Black Sea.

The king who ruled there set Jason more harsh tasks, promising him the Fleece in return. With the help of the king's daughter, Medea, Jason completed them. But the king broke his word. So Medea, a witch, helped Jason to defeat the dragon, seize the Fleece, and set sail for home.

◀WHO WAS ODIN?

Over a thousand years ago, the peoples of northern Europe worshipped their own gods. Chief among them was Odin, god of war.

Early stories told how Odin rode in a flowing cloak and a wide-brimmed hat and led a wild army of ghostly warriors which on stormy nights could be heard galloping across the sky.

Later he became the god who decided the fate of men, especially warriors when they called on him in battle. By Odin's command, dead heroes were burnt on a funeral pyre before joining him in his victory hall of Valhalla.

The warrior god wore a golden helmet. His spear was forged by dwarves and he rode an eight-legged horse called Sleipnir. The wolf and raven were his creatures.

Odin was also god of wisdom and skilled in magic. He often visited the wide world, asking questions. In order to drink from Mimir, the fountain of wisdom, he had sacrificed the sight of one eye.

▶WHO WERE THE VALKYRIES?

According to the legends of northern Europe, maidens called Valkyries decided which heroes should die in battle and join the god Odin in his victory hall of Valhalla.

The Valkyries lived with Odin in Valhalla and acted as his servants and guardians. They carried beer to the warriors feasting at table, keeping their plates and cups filled with meat and drink.

The Valkyries were also sent into battle by Odin. They roamed the battlefield, choosing which heroes should die and which side should win.

Only warriors whose fate it was to die could see these fearsome women in their armour and helmets, brandishing their shields and shining spears.

Once their hero had been chosen, the Valkyries appeared to him and told him of his fate. Then they flew back to Valhalla on their fiery steeds, telling Odin of his new guest's arrival and preparing a place for him at the warriors' table.

▼WHO WAS ROLAND?

A French poem written about 1100 tells the story of Roland, one of the noblest knights to serve Charlemagne, king of the Franks.

The real Roland was Prefect of Brittany and fought with Charlemagne's army against the Arabs in Spain. In 778 the victorious troops marched home to France. But an ambush lay in wait in the mountains. The rearguard, including Roland, were all killed.

From this battle grew up a legend. Charlemagne's knight Ganelon is sent to talk peace with the Saracen (Arab) king. But Ganelon turns traitor and plots with the enemy. He makes sure that Roland is made leader of the rearguard, knowing what fate awaits them.

When the attack comes, Roland fights heroically with his companions. Greatly outnumbered, he refuses at first to call for help. Then, too late, he sounds his horn. When Charlemagne arrives to defeat the enemy, his noblest knights lie slain.

▲WHO LIVED AT CAMELOT?

In the middle ages, story-tellers loved to recount the deeds of brave knights. None were braver or more chivalrous than King Arthur and his Knights of the Round Table, who rode forth from their castle at Camelot.

If there was a real-life Camelot, it was probably a fortress in western Britain. The real King Arthur may have lived around AD 500, fighting to defend Roman Britain against barbarian invaders.

In the stories, Arthur becomes king by drawing a sword from a stone. His sword is called Excalibur, and his counsellor is the wizard Merlin. Arthur's queen Guinevere falls in love with the most valiant of all the Round Table knights, Sir Lancelot. Lancelot's son, the noble Sir Galahad, undertakes the most challenging of all knightly quests, the search for the Holy Grail.

These and many other stories about the Knights of the Round Table became popular in the middle ages and have been told ever since.

▲WHO WAS KING WENCESLAS?

The old kingdom of Bohemia is now part of Czechoslovakia, in eastern Europe. About 921 a Christian boy called Wenceslas came to the throne. Today he is the Czech patron saint.

Wenceslas was brought up by his Christian grandmother, Ludmila. The boy's mother was jealous of Ludmila and had her murdered.

Most Bohemians were pagans. Wenceslas welcomed German missionaries to spread Christianity. But later, German soldiers also arrived. Many nobles turned against Wenceslas, and one day on his way to church he was killed by his brother Boleslav.

Stories were soon told of miracles worked at Wenceslas's tomb, and of the king's great goodness. One tells how he cut wood from the forest to take in secret to widows and orphans. His servant went with him, miraculously kept warm in winter by treading in the saint's footsteps.

▲WHO WAS KNOWN AS EL CID?

The national hero of Spain is Rodrigo Diaz de Vivar, better known by the title 'El Cid Campeador' – the Lord Champion.

El Cid was born in Spain about 1040. At this time Spain was divided between the Moors (Arabs) and Spanish rulers. Both sides quarrelled among themselves. El Cid supported the king of Castile and commanded his army. A brilliant soldier, he won many victories, but was sent into exile suspected of treachery.

He became a mercenary or 'soldier of fortune', leading his own men to take up arms for any who needed his help. Sometimes he fought for the Moors and sometimes for the Spanish.

In 1094 El Cid captured the kingdom of Valencia, which he ruled until he died in 1099. Soon afterwards it fell to the Moors once again.

El Cid was never defeated in battle. His fame passed into legend and stories were told of his heroic adventures.

▼WHO WAS PRESTER JOHN?

At the time of the Crusades, tales were told in Europe of a Christian land in the East, ruled by the priest-king Prester John. Later stories placed the legendary kingdom in Africa.

Prester (Priest) John lived only in legend. In 1145 he was described as a powerful leader, ready to help in the Crusaders' fight for the Holy Land. His own kingdom was said to lie beyond Persia (Iran).

About 1165 a letter from John was supposed to have reached the West, describing the marvels of his lands. The Pope tried to reply, and travellers such as Marco Polo searched for the kingdom. Some stories seemed to link John with the Mongol leader Genghis Khan.

In time the great king's legend moved to Africa, where a king of Ethiopia was known as Prester John.

▲WHO WAS WILLIAM TELL?

The tale of William Tell is legendary. But about 1300 there may have been a man who, like their national hero, helped to free the Swiss from Austrian rule.

The Austrian governor Gessler ordered all the Swiss in Altdorf to bow to a hat set up on a pole in the market square. Tell refused to bow to it and was arrested. Hearing of Tell's skill as a marksman, Gessler offered him his freedom – if he could shoot an apple from his son's head at 150 paces.

Tell shot cleanly. But he had a second arrow ready. Gessler asked why. It was for him, he was told, if Tell had killed his son. Seized again, Tell was taken by boat to Gessler's castle, but a storm blew up and he made his escape. Lying in wait for Gessler, he used the second arrow. Then he led the fight to drive the Austrians out.

◄WHICH PIRATE WAS KNOWN AS BARBAROSSA?

In the 1500s the Barbary coast of North Africa was the base for fierce pirates called corsairs. Fiercest of all was Barbarossa ('Redbeard'), a Turkish captain.

Barbarossa's real name was Khayr ad-Din. He built up a North African stronghold, raiding the Spanish and Portuguese with the backing of the Sultan of Turkey. In 1518 he captured Algiers and turned the city into a nest of pirates.

Barbarossa's ships were mostly galleys (with oars), and captured sailors were condemned to serve as galley slaves. Rich captives were held prisoner until their families paid a ransom.

Governments hired the Barbary pirates to fight for them, and Barbarossa himself became Admiral of the Turkish fleet. He died in 1546, but the corsairs continued to terrorize shipping until Algiers was finally captured by France in the early 1800s. The menace of the Barbary pirates then came to an end.

◄WHO WAS FRANCIS DRAKE?

In the 1500s England and Spain were at war. Spanish ships sailed in fear of Francis Drake, an English captain.

Drake was born in Devon in 1543. He became famous for his bold seamanship, cruising the waters of the Caribbean in search of Spanish galleons.

In 1577 Drake's ship *Pelican* (later renamed the *Golden Hind*) set off on a voyage to South America. This expedition took Drake into the Pacific Ocean, and he did not return home until 1580. He brought back much treasure and was knighted by Queen Elizabeth I.

In 1588 the Spanish Armada sailed to invade England. Drake was playing bowls (so the story goes) when the enemy fleet was sighted. He vowed he would finish the game before fighting the Spaniards. Despite its great strength, the Armada was defeated.

In 1596 Drake died while on another raid against the Spanish in the New World.

◄WHO WERE THE BUCCANEERS?

In the 1600s wild sea rovers hunted ships in the seas off America. French, British and Dutch seafarers sometimes sailed with these buccaneers.

The name came from the French *boucan*, meaning a grill for drying meat to be eaten on board ship. Many buccaneers were pirates, living by raids on merchant ships. Others sold their courage, and their fast ships, to the highest bidder.

The buccaneer Henry Morgan, for instance, ended up as governor of Jamaica and was knighted by the King of England.

By the 1700s the great days of the buccaneers were coming to an end. The French seafarer Jean Lafitte fought for the United States during the war with Britain of 1812. He became a hero but later returned to his old life and sailed off to raid the Spanish in South America, where he died.

In the islands of the Caribbean the buccaneers ruled their ports like kings.

▶ WHO WAS SURCOUF?

Robert Surcouf was called the 'last corsair'. He was a French captain famed for his seamanship and daring.

Surcouf was born in Saint-Malo in 1773. His family wanted him to become a priest but he ran away to sea. By the age of 15 he was sailing the Indian Ocean.

Following the French Revolution, France and Britain went to war. Fast-sailing fighting ships from France fought a hit-and-run war against the British. Surcouf distinguished himself, often defeating enemy ships more powerful than his own.

In 1800 his epic battle with the British ship *Kent* made him a hero. Surcouf's ship, the *Confiance*, captured the *Kent* and with it a large treasure in gold. The French admiralty demanded that Surcouf hand it over to them. Furious, Surcouf hurled the gold into the sea and told the officials to recover it – if they dared.

Surcouf's exploits (despite this incident) made him rich. He died at Saint-Malo in 1827.

▶ WHO WERE ANNE BONNY AND MARY READ?

There were few women pirates on the high seas. Anne Bonny and Mary Read, however, were just as tough as their men shipmates.

The waters of the Caribbean were favourite haunts for pirates in the 1600s and 1700s. There were rich merchant ships to plunder, and plenty of islands with lonely bays in which to anchor, safe from the hangman's noose.

At the sight of the pirate flag, the skull and crossbones, most ships either fled or surrendered. Pirates showed little or no mercy.

Women were seldom found on pirate ships, except as captives. Yet there were women pirates, such as Anne Bonny and Mary Read. Pictures show them armed to the teeth and dressed as men. Both women ran away to sail with the pirate captain John Rackham. Mary Read was captured and died of fever in prison. Anne Bonny was also caught, but her fate thereafter is not known.

▶ WHO WAS ADMIRAL NELSON?

The British admiral Horatio Nelson won brilliant victories, before being killed at the moment of his greatest triumph – the Battle of Trafalgar.

Nelson was born in 1758 and joined the Navy when only 12. He served in a number of warships, losing the sight of his right eye and also his right arm in battle.

In 1798 Nelson defeated the French fleet at the Battle of the Nile, stranding Napoleon's army in Egypt. In 1801 when attacking Copenhagen, he deliberately put his telescope to his blind eye so that he could not see a signal ordering him to break off the attack.

Nelson became a national hero. He was made a viscount, and carried on a famous love affair with Lady Hamilton, the wife of a diplomat. In 1805 he led the British fleet to victory against the French and Spanish at the Battle of Trafalgar. During the battle, Nelson was shot on the deck of his flagship, *Victory*.

◀WHO IS SAID TO HAVE FIDDLED WHILE ROME BURNED?

The Roman emperor Nero is said to have sent early Christians to the lions and to have set fire to Rome. Such stories show him as cruel and mad. But people no longer believe *all* these tales.

Nero became emperor in AD 54, before he was 17. His mother had poisoned any rivals to her son's power, and at first Nero ruled well. He banned bloodthirsty sports from the arena and encouraged poetry, drama and athletics.

But Nero's other side soon showed itself. He led wild riots, took up strange new religions and killed his wife and mother. He thought he was a genius and shocked Roman nobles by appearing on stage.

In 64 fire swept Rome (while Nero was elsewhere). The new building meant higher taxes, and revolts broke out. But Nero just laughed and played his music. The Senate ordered his death, though the emperor probably killed himself.

▶WHO WAS THE MAN IN THE IRON MASK?

In 1698 a masked prisoner was brought to the Bastille in Paris. He was kept in solitary confinement. Who was the mysterious Man in the Iron Mask?

The writer Voltaire coined the name 'Man in the Iron Mask'. He thought the prisoner might be a twin brother of the French King Louis XIV. The prisoner's mask was actually made of velvet, not iron, but the name has stuck ever since.

The mysterious prisoner may have been Count Matthioli, a 'double agent' who had been working for France but was arrested in 1679 for passing secrets to France's enemies.

Some doubts remain. But we do know (because an officer of the Bastille guard recorded it in his diary) that the Man in the Iron Mask died in 1703, still a prisoner.

▶WHO WAS MARY QUEEN OF SCOTS?

Mary was queen of Scotland by birth and queen of France by marriage. She also had a claim to the English throne of her cousin, Elizabeth I.

Mary's father died just before she was born in 1542. Her French mother ruled Scotland for her baby daughter, but was unpopular because she was a Catholic. Most Scots were Protestants.

Mary grew up in France and married the king's heir, but returned to Scotland when he died after a year's reign. Next she married her Catholic cousin Lord Darnley. The Scots lords hated Darnley and one day a mighty blast blew apart the house in which he was staying. Many thought that Mary had known of the plot too.

Later forced to give up her throne to her son James VI, Mary spent the rest of her life in prison. She escaped to England, but was accused of plotting against Elizabeth I and was executed in 1587.

▶ WHO WERE THE BORGIAS?

Few families in history have been so ruthless in their quest for power as the Borgias, who lived in Italy during the 1400s.

The Borgia family came to Italy from Spain and by 1455 had produced a Pope in Calixtus III. His nephew, Rodrigo Borgia, also became Pope, as Alexander VI. Rodrigo was a wholly worldly man – one of the wickedest Popes to rule.

At once he set about making his family rich and powerful (Rodrigo had many children, though priests were forbidden to marry). He made his son Cesare a Cardinal and married his beautiful daughter Lucrezia four times to useful allies. Her first two marriages were annulled and her third husband was killed by her brother. The Borgias were experts at murder (especially poisoning) to gain their ends.

Cesare, who was a brilliant soldier, brought central Italy under Borgia control. But when his father died, the family's power collapsed.

▲ WHO WAS RASPUTIN?

Grigori Rasputin was a Russian priest. He gained a strange power over the Tsar (emperor) of Russia.

Rasputin was born in 1872 in Siberia. He wandered the country as a priest and healer, claiming almost magical powers. In 1905 he came to St Petersburg and won the favour of the Tsar and Tsarina, whose son suffered from a rare blood disease. Rasputin seemed able to help the boy in ways no doctor could.

Through his influence with the Tsarina, Rasputin became the most powerful man in Russia. He used his power badly; he lived wildly, gave the Tsar bad advice, and prevented much-needed reforms. In 1916 a group of nobles murdered him.

But by then Russia was facing defeat in World War I. Within a year the Tsar had been overthrown by the Russian Revolution.

◀ WHO WAS EVA PERON?

From film actress to joint leader of a South American country . . . such was the amazing career of Eva Peron, known to her people as Evita.

Eva Ibarguren (her family name) was born near Buenos Aires in Argentina in 1919. Determined to rise from poverty, she became an actress and made a name as a film star.

In 1945 she married Juan Peron, a former soldier turned politician. In 1946 Peron was elected President of Argentina, and Eva helped bring about reforms such as votes for women and better health services. She was immensely popular, especially among the poor.

Such was Evita's popularity that she would almost certainly have been elected vice-president in 1951, had not army generals persuaded her to stand down. By then she was seriously ill, and on her death in 1952 she was mourned throughout Argentina.

Juan Peron remained President until 1955, and held office again in the 1970s.

▲WHO WAS HIAWATHA?

In the 1500s the Iroquois Indians of North America united against the threat of invasion by white settlers. Their leader was called Hiawatha, meaning 'He Who Makes Rivers'.

There are many stories about Hiawatha, but known facts about his life are few. He was a Mohawk Indian, living in the northwestern part of what is now the USA. Around 1575 he persuaded the various Indian tribes to forget their differences and join together in one Iroquois League.

The Iroquois set up a governing council, and co-operated to safeguard their lands from the white settlers, who were mostly French and English. In this they were largely successful for 200 years, only losing their lands during the American War of Independence.

According to Indian legend, Hiawatha was a man of great wisdom, who studied all the secrets of nature. His story inspired a famous poem, *The Song of Hiawatha* by the American poet Longfellow.

▲WHO WAS POCAHONTAS?

The story goes that in 1608 a young Indian princess saved the life of an English settler. The name of the princess was Pocahontas.

Pocahontas lived in Virginia, at the time when the first English settlers were arriving in North America. Her tribe captured a settler leader called Captain John Smith. Just as the captive was about to be put to death, Pocahontas rushed forward to shield him from the executioner and begged her father to spare the white man.

The chief agreed, and Captain Smith was allowed to go free. Later, Pocahontas herself was captured and held hostage by the settlers. She eventually married one of them, John Rolfe, and in 1616 he brought her to England. There she met the King and Queen. Sadly, Pocahontas died just before she was due to sail back to Virginia.

The story of how Pocahontas saved John Smith's life may not be true. But she certainly helped make peace between the Indians and the settlers.

▼WHO WAS DANIEL BOONE?

In the 1700s white settlers began moving westward across America. One of the first frontiersmen was the hunter and trapper, Daniel Boone.

Boone was born in 1734 in Pennsylvania. He helped open up a new trail for settlers through the Cumberland Gap in the Appalachian Mountains. The Indians fought against the intruders, and Boone's son Jim was killed in one fight.

Like other frontiersmen, Daniel Boone lived by hunting and trapping wild animals. But he also founded settlements; one was called Boonesborough after him, and his own wife and daughter were the first white women to live in Kentucky.

In 1778 Boone was captured by Pawnee Indians. The Indian chief adopted him as a son! Later, he fought the British during the American War of Independence. He travelled west, exploring the Ohio River and Louisiana.

Daniel Boone died in 1820, famous not only in America, but even in far-off Europe.

▼WHO WAS DAVY CROCKETT?

One Tennessee frontiersman became a US Congressman. His tall stories of backwoods life made him famous and his death at the siege of the Alamo made him a hero. His name was Davy Crockett.

Davy Crockett was born in 1786. He had little schooling and spent much of his time in the mountains, hunting bears and fighting Indians. Then he became a politician and was elected to the US Congress.

In 1835, defeated in an election, he turned his back on politics and headed for Texas to help the Texans in their fight for independence. (Texas was then ruled by Mexico.) In 1836 Davy Crockett was one of 200 defenders of the Alamo mission, fighting off a Mexican army. In one of the most famous battles in US history all the defenders were killed.

The Texans won their freedom in the end, and later joined the United States. Davy Crockett became an American legend.

▲WHO WAS GERONIMO?

As white settlers moved west across America, they pushed the Indians off their tribal lands. Among the Indians who fought the invaders most fiercely was the Apache chief Geronimo.

Geronimo's people, the Chiricahua Apache, lived in Arizona in the southwest USA. His real name was Gogathlay, or 'One Who Yawns', and he was born in 1829.

Geronimo fought the Mexicans and the Americans to defend the Apaches' hunting grounds. In 1874 the US Army moved the Apaches to a barren reservation, but Geronimo and a small band of warriors continued to fight. He eluded the Army until 1886, when he agreed to surrender.

He spent the rest of his life under guard in Oklahoma. He tried the white man's ways, but never accepted them, and died in 1908. The US soldier who knew him best, Colonel George Crook, called Geronimo 'one of the greatest Americans that ever lived'.

▲WHO WAS KNOWN AS CALAMITY JANE?

Women living in the Wild West had to be tough. None came tougher than Calamity Jane who could out-shoot (and out-drink) most men in the frontier towns.

Calamity Jane was not her real name. She was born Martha Canary (also known as Martha Burk), probably in 1852. She lived in Deadwood, South Dakota, which at that time was the kind of rough and rowdy Western town later made familiar in cowboy films.

Calamity Jane often dressed in men's clothes. She rode and shot like an expert, and loved wild drinking sessions in saloons. Her real-life adventures were exaggerated in numerous Western novels. Indeed, she eventually toured with a Wild West show, showing off her skill with a rifle.

Calamity Jane died in 1903. By then the exciting days of the Wild West were coming to an end. The legend of Calamity Jane, fighter for justice (which she did not really deserve), lived on.

◀WHO WAS SPARTACUS?

In the Roman Empire, slaves did most of the work. Some slaves were treated well; but many were not. In 71 BC there was a slaves' revolt, led by a gladiator called Spartacus.

Spartacus was born in Thrace (modern Bulgaria). He was forced to serve in the Roman army, ran away but was caught and punished. He was sent to train as a gladiator. His likely fate was to fight and die in the arena.

Spartacus and a band of fellow gladiators broke out of their training camp, and took to the countryside as outlaws. Other slaves flocked to join the rebels. Leading this slaves' army, Spartacus won several battles against Roman legions sent to crush the revolt.

The slaves hoped to escape to their native lands, but after two years they were finally defeated. Spartacus was one of many who died in battle. Thousands of others were put to death by being crucified.

◀DID ROBIN HOOD REALLY EXIST?

For over 600 years stories have been told of the English outlaw Robin Hood, who 'robbed the rich to help the poor'. Perhaps a real-life outlaw gave rise to the legend.

The real Robin Hood may have been a Saxon, who lost his land following the Norman Conquest of England in 1066. Some stories tell of him living in Sherwood Forest, Nottinghamshire, at the time of King Richard I (1157-1199). So two, or more, real outlaws may lie behind the legend.

In the stories Robin Hood is the best archer in England. His outlaw band includes Maid Marian, Friar Tuck (a fat priest), and Little John (a giant of a man). The arch enemy of the outlaws is the Sheriff of Nottingham.

There are several places in northern England named after Robin Hood. So maybe he was a real person. No-one can be sure.

◀WHO WAS JESSE JAMES?

One of the most celebrated outlaws of the American West was Jesse James. He robbed banks and held up trains. He was finally shot dead by one of his own gang.

Jesse James was from Missouri, and fought for the South during the US Civil War. When the South was defeated at the end of the war, Jesse and his brother Frank turned to crime.

For 16 years the James gang robbed and murdered. They claimed they were still fighting for the South, as outlaws. But in fact they were no better than the many other bandits who attacked banks, stagecoaches and railroads.

Eventually, a large reward was offered for Jesse's capture, dead or alive. In 1882 he was shot dead by Robert Ford, one of his own gang who claimed the reward. Jesse James became the hero of many Western books and films. His brother Frank was tried, but freed and spent the rest of his life quietly, as a farmer.

▶ WHO WAS NED KELLY?

In Australia during the 1800s outlaws were known as 'bushrangers'. Ned Kelly was the last, and most famous, of the bushrangers.

Kelly was born in 1855 in the state of Victoria. He formed an outlaw gang with his brother Dan, raiding rich landowners and stealing horses. The gang's daring robberies soon made them famous. Some of the poorer farmers admired Kelly as a kind of Australian Robin Hood.

For several years the Kelly gang escaped the law. Then their luck ran out. They took over a township called Glenrowan, but were surrounded by police troopers. In the gun battle, all the gang were shot dead, except Ned Kelly who was wearing homemade armour for protection. He was wounded and captured. On November 11, 1880 he was hanged in Melbourne.

Ned Kelly became an Australian folk hero but some of the stories about him overlook his worst crimes.

▶ WHO WERE PANCHO VILLA AND EMILIANO ZAPATA?

Villa and Zapata are two great names in modern Mexican history. Both were guerrilla leaders who dreamt of a better life for the poor people of Mexico.

Villa was born in 1878; Zapata in 1879. Both were the sons of poor farmers. Few Mexicans owned land, and there was much injustice. Villa became an outlaw for killing the owner of the estate on which his family worked. Zapata called for the land to be shared fairly among all the people.

Villa and Zapata led guerrilla bands in the war to bring about a revolution in Mexico which began in 1910. It was a bitter struggle, with many disagreements between the revolutionary leaders. A new republic was created, but neither Villa nor Zapata lived long enough to see it. In 1919 Zapata was murdered and four years later the same fate overtook Villa.

Today they are honoured as founders of modern Mexico.

▶ WHO WAS AL CAPONE?

In the 1920s and 1930s gangster mobs controlled crime in the USA. One of the most notorious gang bosses was Al Capone.

The gangsters took control of crime in several US cities during the era of Prohibition (1920 to 1933). The government banned the sale of alcohol. As a result of this illegal breweries and drinking clubs sprang up. The Mafia, a secret organization made up of mainly Italian 'family' gangs, took control of the business.

From 1925 to 1931 Capone was boss of the Chicago gangs. He was a ruthless criminal. Dreadful killings, such as the St Valentine's Day Massacre, were carried out on his orders. The authorities finally jailed him, not for murder but for a tax offence, and he died in 1947.

Most other gang leaders died violently in bloody wars between rival gangs. The Federal Bureau of Investigation or FBI was set up by the US government to fight organized crime.

◀WHO WAS KNOWN AS 'THE LADY WITH THE LAMP'?

British soldiers wounded in the Crimean War called the nurse in charge of their hospital 'the lady with the lamp'. Today she is known as the founder of modern nursing, Florence Nightingale.

When the Nightingale family heard that Florence wanted to be a nurse, they were shocked. Few women had jobs in 1845 and nursing was not a respectable career. But Florence had her way. She worked with nursing nuns in Germany and France before taking charge of a London hospital in 1853.

A year later she was in Scutari, in Turkey, nursing wounded soldiers. Hospital conditions so horrified her that she began at once to reorganize nursing methods. Thankful soldiers seeing her pass by at night named her 'the lady with the lamp'.

To help her work continue, in 1860 Florence set up the Nightingale School for Nurses, the first of its kind in the world.

▶WHICH BLACK AMERICAN WAS KNOWN AS THE MOSES OF HER PEOPLE?

As Moses led the Israelites from slavery in Egypt, so Harriet Tubman guided slaves from the Southern states of America to freedom in the North.

Harriet Tubman was born a slave in Maryland about 1820. In 1849 she escaped, making her way to the North, where slavery had ended. She was helped by an organization that passed slaves along a secret route to freedom. Harriet later joined this 'underground' group herself.

After freeing members of her own family, she went back to the South time after time. With a price on her head, there was danger in every 'run' and 'General' Tubman urged on timid followers with a loaded gun! In all, she led 300 slaves to freedom.

Harriet was a nurse and a spy for the North in its Civil War with the South. When the North won, all American slaves became free.

◀WHO FOUNDED THE RED CROSS?

The Red Cross brings help in time of human need, in peace or war. It was begun by international agreement in 1863. But the idea was that of Henri Dunant, a young Swiss banker.

In 1859, in north Italy, Austrians and French fought the Battle of Solferino. Men lay wounded in the fierce heat and among those who saw their suffering was Henri Dunant.

Dunant wrote a book about the battle and suggested that a society to help wounded soldiers be set up in every country. In 1863 a meeting in Geneva brought the first Red Cross societies into being.

Today the Red Cross is at work all over the world. It gives emergency aid in time of disaster, helps prisoners of war and runs welfare schemes. Its red cross on a white background is a symbol respected by all nations. In Muslim countries the sign is a red crescent.

▶ WHO WAS ALBERT SCHWEITZER?

Teacher, philosopher and musician: Albert Schweitzer was a man of many talents. Above all he is remembered for his work as a missionary doctor in Africa.

Schweitzer was born in 1875 in Alsace (then in Germany, now part of France). A brilliant student, he became a professor of theology and wrote several books about Christianity. He was equally famous as an organist.

In 1905 Schweitzer gave up university work to train as a medical doctor. He and his wife then travelled to West Africa and built a missionary hospital at Lambarene in Gabon.

During World War I all German citizens had to leave French territories overseas. Schweitzer returned to find his hospital in ruins. He rebuilt it, and later set up a leper colony nearby. He lived at Lambarene, caring for the sick, until his death in 1965. He won the Nobel Peace Prize in 1952.

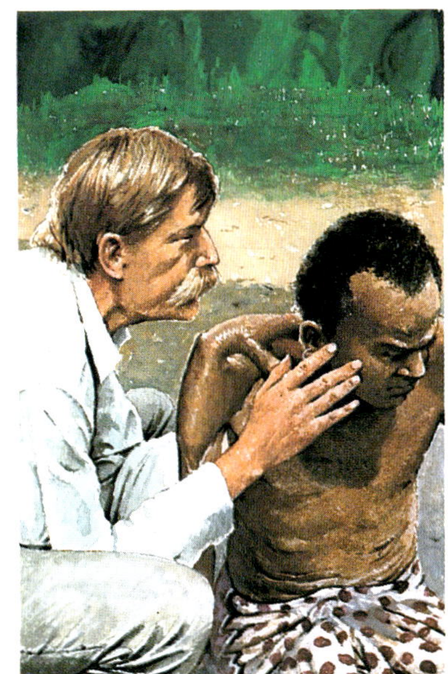

◀ WHO WAS HELEN KELLER?

After an illness as a baby, Helen Keller was left blind, deaf and dumb. With the aid of a devoted teacher, she mastered her handicaps and worked to help other blind and deaf people.

Helen was born in the USA in 1880. After six years in a silent, dark world, a teacher was found from the Perkins School for the Blind in Boston. Her name was Anne Sullivan.

Anne tamed the wild young girl and taught her how to 'speak'. First she tapped out the sign alphabet on her hand; then she tapped out the names of objects. In two years, Helen could read and write in Braille, the special writing used by the blind. She learnt to talk, by touching Anne's throat and feeling her voice vibrate. Then Helen made her own voice do the same.

Helen Keller went to college, with Anne at her side, and spent her life writing and working for the deaf and blind throughout the world.

▶ WHO IS KNOWN AS MOTHER TERESA?

A Catholic nun gave up her work teaching in an Indian school to live among the poor and sick of a city's slums. She is known as Mother Teresa of Calcutta and has been called a living saint.

Agnes Gonxha Bojaxhiu was born in 1910 in Skopje, now in Yugoslavia. She became a nun, studied in Ireland, and went to teach in Calcutta, India. Travelling on a train one night, she heard a voice telling her to leave the convent and help the poor.

She wore a sari and went barefoot in the poorest slums of Calcutta. In 1948 the Church let her set up a new order of nuns, called the Missionaries of Charity.

For 30 years Mother Teresa and her nuns have saved babies left on rubbish tips, looked after lepers and cared for the sick and dying. By 1979 her order had nearly 200 branches throughout the world, and she was awarded the Nobel Peace Prize.

THE ARTS AND ENTERTAINMENT

▼WHO WROTE *THE EPIC OF GILGAMESH?*

***The Epic of Gilgamesh* is an ancient collection of stories first told in the area of the Middle East known as Mesopotamia. We do not know who first wrote them down, only that this happened in about 2000 BC.**

Like all epic poems, it tells the story of a hero and his adventures. In this case it is Gilgamesh, a king in Babylon, and his friend Enkidu. The stories probably go back to about 3000 BC, but at first they were passed on by word of mouth. Eventually they were written down on clay tablets.

There were five poems. One is especially interesting as it tells the story of a great flood, and how one family survived by building an ark. This is believed to be the basis for the Bible story of Noah.

▼WHO WAS THE AUTHOR OF THE *ILIAD* AND THE *ODYSSEY*?

The *Iliad* and the *Odyssey* are two great Greek epic poems which tell the story of the siege of the city of Troy, and the events that took place afterwards. Tradition has it that they were written by Homer, a blind singer from the Greek island of Chios.

We know very little about Homer – we are not even sure he existed at all! In fact, the *Iliad* and the *Odyssey* may have been written by two different people.

But if Homer did exist, he was probably a travelling story-teller who sang these stories to the music of a lyre.

Until Homer's time these tales had been handed down through the ages by word of mouth. He wrote them down for the first time in about 600 BC.

▼WHO WAS SAPPHO?

Sappho was a poet of ancient Greece, from the island of Lesbos in the Aegean sea. She is the only woman poet of her time who is remembered today.

Sappho lived between 610 and 580 BC. She was an educated woman from a noble family.

We do not know very much more about her, except that she had a daughter named Cleis.

Much of her work was love-poetry addressed to other women. It was collected together from about 300 to 200 BC, but by the 8th and 9th centuries only a few fragments of it were left.

She was almost forgotten for many centuries, although in her own time she was so famous that her portrait was put on coins and vases and her style copied by many other poets.

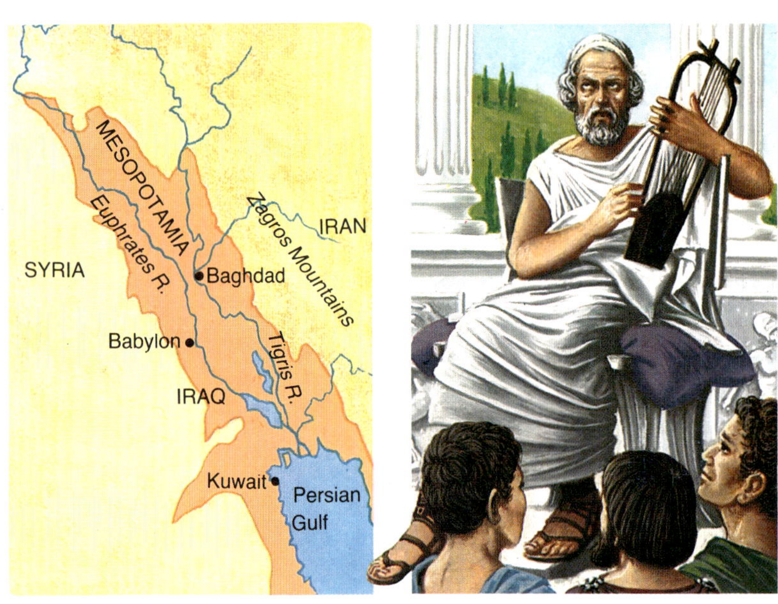

▼WHO WAS THE AUTHOR OF FABLES ABOUT ANIMALS?

The traditional Greek fables about animals (short stories with a moral at the end) are supposed to have been written by a crippled freed slave named Aesop, who lived in the 5th century BC.

Many scholars believe that Aesop was not a real person at all – it was just a custom in ancient Greece to call the author of animal fables 'Aesop'. The stories were probably traditional and were passed on by word of mouth. The story of their author also became a part of that tradition, and was probably not true.

The stories themselves are still popular. The picture shows the tale of the fox who, when he could not reach a bunch of grapes, decided they must be sour anyway.

The versions we know today are based on the work of a Roman writer named Phaedrus, himself a freed slave, who lived at about the time of Christ. But the stories were collected and written down much earlier, about the 4th century BC.

▼WHO IS THE HERO OF THE *RAMAYAMA*?

The *Ramayama* is a great Indian epic poem. The hero is Rama, the king of Oudh in northern India. Rama is supposed to have been the God Vishnu who took human form and came down to earth to save the world from evil.

The *Ramayama* (meaning 'the deeds of Rama') was written by the poet Valmiki in about 300 BC, in an early Indian language called Sanskrit.

The poem's seven books tell the story of Rama and how he won the hand of Sita, the daughter of another king, in a contest. The couple were happy at first, but Rama was driven out of his kingdom and was forced to live in the forest with Sita and his half-brother Laksana.

While they were there, the demon king Ravana of Lanka (Sri Lanka) carried Sita off to his kingdom. Rama and Laksana managed to get her back with the help of Sugriva, the king of the monkeys and his general Hanuman. Rama and Sita returned to Oudh, and Rama regained his throne.

▼WHO WAS VIRGIL?

Virgil – whose full name was Publius Vergilius Maro – was a Roman poet, whose most famous work was the *Aeneid*. This is a great epic poem about the fall of Troy and the beginning of the Roman nation.

Virgil was born in 70 BC near Mantua in Italy. Because he was lucky enough to have a rich patron to support him, he was able to devote himself to writing throughout his life. His first poems were about the countryside, but it was his last, the epic *Aeneid*, that he is remembered for.

This tells the story of the fall of Troy, and how Aeneas escaped, leading a band of followers to Italy, where they were able to settle.

The poem tells of their adventures during the journey – including crossing the mythical river Styx in order to reach the Underworld.

Virgil died in 19 BC, after a trip to Greece, where he caught a fever. He had wanted the *Aeneid* burned when he died, but the emperor insisted it was published.

▶WHO WAS OMAR KHAYYAM?

Omar Khayyam was a Persian poet, astronomer and a brilliant scholar who lived in the 11th century AD. He is most famous as a poet, and a collection of his work, called the *Rubaiyat*, was translated into English by the 19th century poet, Edward Fitzgerald.

Omar Khayyam was born in the city of Nishapur (now called Neyshabur) in Persia (present-day Iran).

Because he was such a talented scholar, he was appointed to the job of royal astronomer, and asked to modernise the Persian calendar. Later, he worked with other astronomers to build an observatory in the city of Isfahan. In his own day, he was famous as a writer on science, history, law, medicine and, especially, mathematics.

He was not thought of as an important poet. In fact, not all scholars agree that the *Rubaiyat* is really his. In any case, it was not published until 200 years after his death.

◀WHO WROTE *THE TALE OF GENJI*?

***The Tale of Genji* is an 11th century book from Japan which is sometimes said to be the very first novel ever written. Its author was a woman – Murasaki Shikibu.**

Whether or not *The Tale of Genji* is the first ever novel, it is the first important one.

It was written at a time when it was common for the ladies at the court of the Japanese emperor to write diaries. Murasaki herself wrote one before she wrote *The Tale of Genji*. She also wrote a short story which included some poetry – *Izumi Shikibu nikki*. She wrote *The Tale of Genji* in about 1010. It was an immediate success.

The story is of the life and loves of Prince Genji. He loves several women, and each one reacts differently to him. The book was popular for centuries afterwards – which was not always a good thing. Many writers felt they had to produce very similar books, rather than something new and different.

▶WHO TOLD STORIES FOR 1001 NIGHTS?

There was once a princess in Arabia who saved herself from death by telling stories for 1001 nights.

The story tells of a cruel king named Shahryar who had his wife put to death, and then married a new wife every day and had her put to death too. Eventually he married Sharazad, the daughter of his chief minister, who planned to put an end to all this killing.

On her wedding night, she began to tell the king a story. But when she reached the most exciting part of it, she stopped, and said if he wanted to hear the end he would have to let her live another day. This went on for 1001 nights, until the king gave up his plan. Among the stories that Sharazad told were those of *Sindbad the Sailor* and *Aladdin*. The stories are traditional, and come from many parts of the Middle and Far East. The first written copy was made in Arabic in about 1000 AD. The stories are known as the 'Arabian Nights' Entertainment'.

◄WHO WROTE *THE DIVINE COMEDY*?

***The Divine Comedy* – which many scholars think is one of the most important pieces of literature produced in medieval Europe – was written by the poet Dante Aligheri in his own language, Italian.**

Dante was born in Florence in 1265, but after getting involved in the politics of the city was forced to leave. After much travelling he settled in the city of Ravenna.

One of the most important aspects of *The Divine Comedy* is that it was written in a modern language. Scholars at the time thought that any serious poetry should be written in Latin.

The poem is in three parts. In the first, the poet – Dante himself – describes a journey through Hell (the *Inferno*) with the poet Virgil as his guide. Next – still in the company of Virgil – he visits Purgatory.

In the final part – this time with Beatrice, a woman he idealised – he visits Heaven, and even glimpses God.

►WHO WAS PETRARCH?

Petrarch was a scholar and poet who had an enormous influence on European poetry from the fourteenth century onwards.

Petrarch's full name was Francesco Petrarca. He lived from 1304 to 1374. Although he was an Italian, he spent much of his life in France.

He wrote more than 400 poems of his own – 366 of which are in a collection called *The Book of Songs*. Many of these are written to a woman called Laura. We do not know if she was a real person, or just Petrarch's ideal woman. He was especially important because he set out firm rules for writing poetry, including the number of lines to be used.

As well as writing poetry, Petrarch spent much of his life researching Latin poetry – though he himself had followed Dante's example and written in Italian. It is thanks to Petrarch's work that the poetry of the Romans Livy and Cicero was rediscovered. Without him, they might have been forgotten altogether.

◄WHO WROTE *THE CANTERBURY TALES*?

***The Canterbury Tales* are a collection of stories in verse which are supposed to have been told by the different members of a party of 14th century pilgrims on their way from London to Canterbury. In fact, all the stories are the work of the English poet Geoffrey Chaucer.**

Chaucer lived between 1342 and 1400. He had a varied life – he served as a soldier and worked as a diplomat and a civil servant as well as being a poet. *The Canterbury Tales* is his best known work, but not his only one. His romance about the Trojan war – *Troilus and Criseyde* – is still read today but nothing he wrote has remained as popular as *The Canterbury Tales* – which in fact Chaucer never finished.

The stories are designed to reflect the characters of the tellers – they range from the bawdy miller's tale to the knight's story of honour and chivalry. Today, modern English versions of his work are still widely read.

◀WHO WAS DON QUIXOTE?

Don Quixote was the hero of a 17th century novel written by the Spanish author, Miguel de Cervantes.

Cervantes lived between 1547 and 1616. He had an adventurous life – serving first as a soldier (when he was captured by the Turks and kept prisoner) and later as a government servant.

His 'hero', Don Quixote, has adventures of a very different kind. For poor Don Quixote is described as an eccentric old man who decides to become a knight and take on deeds of daring, as in the days of old. So he puts on a suit of rusty old armour, mounts his old horse and sets out with his faithful companion, Sancho Panza (mounted on a donkey).

Being old and short-sighted, Don Quixote makes many mistakes and misunderstands a great many situations. One of the best known stories in the book tells how he mistakes a row of windmills for giants, and sets about fighting them! At the end, Don Quixote settles down quietly at home.

◀WHO MADE THE FIRST COLLECTIONS OF FAIRY TALES?

Many of the fairy tales we know today are so old that we have no idea who first made them up – but we do know that the first collection of European traditional stories was made by the French writer, Charles Perrault, in 1697. Two collectors of fairy tales were the German brothers, Jacob Carl and Wilhelm Carl Grimm.

Perrault's collection of stories was made specifically for children – his own children, in fact. He called them *Tales of the Past* and among the stories he recorded were many that are still favourites today – such as *Puss in Boots* and *Bluebeard*.

The Brothers Grimm (as they became known) were much more serious, scientific collectors of folklore. They tried to record stories just as they heard them. Their work, aimed at adults as well as children, took place between 1812 and 1822. Among their tales were *Hansel and Gretel* (left) and *Tom Thumb*.

◀WHO WAS ROBINSON CRUSOE?

Robinson Crusoe was the name of the hero of an adventure story about a shipwrecked sailor. It was written by the Englishman Daniel Defoe in 1719.

The story tells how Robinson Crusoe was cast up on a desert island, the only survivor of a shipwreck. It goes on to describe how he managed to live alone for many years, and later how he befriended a local man, whom he called Friday.

The idea of a poor castaway having to fend for himself on a desert island has always been popular. Defoe got the idea for the story from real-life tales of shipwrecked sailors – in particular the story of a man named Alexander Selkirk, very like Robinson Crusoe, who was well-known in Defoe's day.

Robinson Crusoe was not Defoe's only work. He was a journalist, who wrote political pamphlets (which sometimes got him into trouble) and the author of several other novels, including *Moll Flanders*, and *A Journal of the Plague Year*.

▶WHO WROTE *GULLIVER'S TRAVELS*?

Gulliver's *Travels* is a satirical story about the adventures of a ship's doctor named Lemuel Gulliver. It was written by Jonathan Swift – a clergyman and scholar who lived from 1667 to 1745.

Swift was born in Ireland and educated at Trinity College Dublin. After spending the early part of his adult life in England, he eventually became Dean of St Patrick's Cathedral, Dublin. His writing is bitterly satirical and he was often very unpopular. Even *Gulliver's Travels*, though it is often told as an enjoyable story for children, was written he said, 'to vex the world'. It is in fact a disguised attack on the unpleasant aspects of life and politics in his own day.

Apart from the familiar story of Gulliver's capture by the tiny people of Lilliput, the book tells of other adventures, including a trip to Brobdingnag, a land of giants, and to a land where horse-like creatures rule.

▶WHO WAS CANDIDE?

Candide is the name of the hero of a satirical novel by the French writer Voltaire, who lived from 1694 to 1778.

Voltaire's real name was Francois Marie Arouet. He spent much of his life fighting tyranny, attacking those he thought were wrong with cruel satire.

Candide is his best known work. It tells the story of a young man who, influenced by his tutor Pangloss, is convinced that we live in 'the best of all possible worlds'. Voltaire attacked this philosophy of optimism by describing how Candide, after being involved in many horrific adventures, involving rape, murder, war and an earthquake, eventually abandons this belief and comes to the conclusion that the best we can do is go and 'cultivate our own gardens'.

Voltaire himself was at one point a prisoner in the famous Bastille in Paris, and later he lived in exile in England. He eventually settled in Switzerland.

▶WHO CREATED FRANKENSTEIN'S MONSTER?

The story of the scientist Frankenstein, and the monster he made out of parts of other humans, was written by Mary Shelley, and was published in 1818.

Mary Shelley was born in 1797 and died in 1851.

When she was only 17, she fell in love with the poet Percy Bysshe Shelley. Although he was already married, the couple ran away together to Switzerland, where they lived for a while with the poet Lord Byron. When Shelley's wife died in 1816, Mary was able to marry Shelley, but he died only six years later in a sailing accident.

She spent much of her life editing her husband's work. She continued to write herself, published a collection of stories and kept a journal. But *Frankenstein* is her most famous work. It tells how the monster made by Frankenstein saw so much cruelty and evil in the world that he turned against it.

◀WHO WAS ALESSANDRO MANZONI?

Alessandro Manzoni was a 19th century Italian writer, whose novel, *I Promessi Sposi*, is one of the most important works in Italian literature.

Manzoni was born in 1785 and died in 1873. He was a devout Roman Catholic, and this had a deep effect on his view of the world and therefore on his writing. In his own time he was known as a poet, but today he is remembered for his great novel, *I Promessi Sposi*. This is set in 17th century Lombardy and tells how a wicked local tyrant, Don Rodrigo, tries to prevent a young peasant couple, Renzo and Lucia, from marrying, but without success.

Manzoni wove historical events into the story in a way that was quite new in Italian literature. The kind of language he wrote in was also important. It was a very pure form of the Tuscan dialect, which became the model for Italian writing for the next hundred years.

▶WHO WAS MOBY DICK?

Moby Dick was a great white whale, whose story was written by the American, Herman Melville.

The story of Moby Dick is really the story of Captain Ahab, an old seafarer who spends his life trying to capture the great whale. Ahab has lost a leg in his hunt for Moby Dick, and finding him is an obsession. At the end of the story, Ahab's ship is lost and there is only one survivor.

Much of *Moby Dick* tells of the dangers and difficulties of whaling in the 19th century – before the days of factory ships – when the only way to catch a whale was for men to go out from the whaling ships in small boats in the icy sea and harpoon it.

Melville, who lived from 1819 to 1891, knew much about whaling, for he had been out on the ships himself and had had many adventures – including being shipwrecked and taking part in a mutiny. Today we remember him mainly for *Moby Dick*, though he wrote other stories.

◀WHO WAS VICTOR HUGO?

Victor Hugo was a French poet, dramatist and novelist who is remembered today for two great novels – *The Hunchback of Notre Dame* and *Les Misérables*.

Victor Hugo was born in 1802 and spent much of his childhood travelling with his father, an army officer.

His career as writer started in about 1822, when he began to write plays. *The Hunchback of Notre Dame*, a novel set in medieval Paris, appeared in 1831. Hugo was involved in politics which, in 1851, led to him having to leave France and live in exile for nearly 20 years.

Throughout this time, when he lived mainly in Jersey, he went on writing, and produced two books of poetry – *The Contemplations* and *The Legend of the Centuries* – as well as his greatest novel, *Les Misérables*. This tells the story of Jean Valjean, an escaped convict who tries to lead an honest and useful life.

At the end of his life, Hugo returned to France, where he died in 1885.

▶WHO WERE THE THREE MUSKETEERS?

The Three Musketeers were the creations of the 19th century French writer, Alexandre Dumas. The musketeers, Porthos, Athos and Aramis, together with their friend d'Artagnan, were supposed to have been adventurers in 17th century France.

Dumas lived from 1803 to 1870. We know him as Dumas *père*, since his son was also a writer. Dumas *père's* father (himself the son of a nobleman and a black woman from the Caribbean) was an army general. Dumas, who could hardly read as a young man, went to Paris and became first a playwright and then a popular historical novelist.

Dumas is remembered today both for *The Three Musketeers* and for his melodramatic *The Count of Monte Cristo* – the tale of mysterious ex-prisoner Edmond Dantes, bent on revenge for his unjust captivity.

◀WHO WAS HANS CHRISTIAN ANDERSEN?

Hans Christian Andersen was a Danish writer of children's stories, whose work includes such favourites as *The Ugly Duckling* and *The Little Mermaid*.

Hans Andersen was born in 1805 and died in 1875. Although his family were poor, he managed to get into university, and afterwards became a writer.

His first book of children's stories had in it some of his best known – including *The Tinderbox* and *The Princess and the Pea* (left) – but it was years before he was really successful.

He based his stories on traditional tales, but they were very different from the collections of people such as the Brothers Grimm. Instead of being about ogres and witches, many of Andersen's stories such as *The Constant Tin Soldier* and *The Little Fir Tree*, reflect his own rather sad and lonely life.

We know from his letters that he was a sensitive and witty man.

▶WHO WAS HONORÉ DE BALZAC?

Honoré de Balzac was a French writer whose best known work is a series of about 100 novels and short stories to which he gave the overall title of *The Human Comedy*.

Balzac was born in Tours in 1799. In 1816 he left for Paris where he studied law for three years before deciding to become a writer. He spent much of his life investing in risky ventures and had to write hard to pay his debts.

His novels, which are about provincial and Parisian life, include characters from many walks of life and cover themes such as fatherly love, greed and envy as well as dealing with many other aspects of life and politics in France.

The Human Comedy is a complicated work, with more than 2000 characters in it, many appearing in more than one novel. The best-known titles include *Old Goriot* and *Cousin Bette*. Balzac died in 1850. The picture shows a statue of Balzac by Rodin.

▼WHO WAS CHARLES DICKENS?

Many people think that Charles Dickens was the greatest of all English novelists. His books include *The Pickwick Papers*, *A Christmas Carol*, *Little Dorrit* and many others.

Dickens was born in 1812. His early life was spent in poverty and his family were at one time in a debtors prison.

He used this experience in his novels – especially *David Copperfield*, which is partly the story of his own life.

His first success was with *The Pickwick Papers*, which was published in weekly parts in a magazine in 1837.

He went on to write many more novels – most of them successful and many still very popular today. Although his early work was comic, his later books are much more serious, and describe the poverty, cruelty and corruption of 19th century England.

Late in his life, he spent much of his time travelling, giving readings from his novels. Dickens died in 1870.

▼WHO WROTE THE FIRST DETECTIVE STORIES?

The first detective stories were the work of the American writer, Edgar Allen Poe. He actually set the stories in Paris, and created a Frenchman, C. Auguste Dupin, as his hero.

Poe lived from 1809 to 1849. He worked mainly as a magazine editor – a very successful one who really seemed to understand what his public wanted to read. His own stories were often spine-chillers, such as *The Fall of the House of Usher*.

His detective Auguste Dupin first appears in a story called *The Murders in the Rue Morgue*, as the man who solves the mystery of a series of murders done by someone with apparently superhuman strength – who turns out to be a giant ape. Another story about M. Dupin – *The Purloined Letter* – is about blackmail in high society. In his own day, Poe was famous as a poet and critic. But today he is thought of mainly as a master of the short story who influenced many later writers.

▼WHO WERE THE BRONTË SISTERS?

Charlotte, Emily and Anne Brontë were all English novelists. Charlotte (1816-1854) is remembered best for *Jane Eyre*, and Emily (1818-1849) for what is often called a masterpiece, *Wuthering Heights*. Anne (1820-1849) wrote two novels – *The Tenant of Wildfell Hall*, and *Agnes Grey*.

The three sisters and their brother Branwell spent most of their lives in their father's house, the parsonage at Haworth, on the bleak Yorkshire moors.

They started writing as children, creating fantasy kingdoms called Angria and Gondal. As adults, they occasionally worked away from home as teachers.

The wild countryside around their home was a strong influence on their novels, especially Emily's *Wuthering Heights*. Both Anne and Emily died young, of consumption (TB) while Charlotte, who married, lived only a little longer, and eventually died in pregnancy.

▼WHO WROTE *ALICE'S ADVENTURES IN WONDERLAND*?

Lewis Carroll, whose real name was Charles Lutwidge Dodgson, was a brilliant scholar and mathematician. But we remember him as the author of two of the most popular children's books ever written in English, *Alice's Adventures in Wonderland* and *Through the Looking Glass*.

Lewis Carroll lived from 1832 to 1898. He was educated at Christchurch College Oxford, where he spent most of his adult life. He never married, and had no children of his own, but he enjoyed their company and loved telling them stories.

The story of Alice, who followed a rabbit down his burrow and into a topsy-turvy underground world, was first told in 1862, to Alice Liddell, the daughter of a friend.

Alice asked Lewis Carroll to write it down and a novelist friend who happened to see the manuscript persuaded its author to get it published. It appeared in 1865 – with illustrations by Tenniel, a popular cartoonist at the time. The book was immediately very successful, and Lewis Carroll followed it with *Through the Looking Glass* in 1872. In this story Alice enters a world where everything is back to front.

Lewis Carroll also published several books on mathematics, under his real name, and was a good amateur photographer.

▼WHO WROTE THE FIRST SCIENCE FICTION STORIES?

The first science fiction stories were the work of the French writer, Jules Verne. Although he died in 1905 (he was born in 1828) and saw almost nothing of modern technology, he still managed to write about helicopters and moon rockets.

Jules Verne was not a scientist, or an adventurer. The nearest he came to doing anything nearly as exciting as his fictional characters was to make one trip in a balloon!

The stories for which he is now so famous were first published in serial form in a magazine and were given the general title of *Voyages Extraordinaires*. These included *A Voyage to the Centre of the Earth*, *Twenty Thousand Leagues Under the Sea* and several others. In his imaginary journeys he foresaw travel by rocket, the development of the submarine and the invention of television.

He even managed to describe weightlessness, long before any astronauts had travelled in space!

▼WHO WROTE *WAR AND PEACE*?

***War and Peace* – often said to be one of the greatest novels ever written – was the work of the 19th century Russian writer, Leo Tolstoy.**

Tolstoy lived from 1828 to 1910. He was a nobleman, with a large family estate south of Moscow.

But although he was wealthy, his sympathies lay with the poverty-stricken peasantry. As he grew older, he became deeply religious and lived very simply.

In his own lifetime he was admired as a philosopher as well as a writer, but today he is remembered mainly for two great works – *War and Peace* and *Anna Karenina*.

War and Peace, set in the early 1800s, describes the lives of a group of aristocratic families and the effects on them of great historical events, such as Napoleon's attack on the city of Moscow.

Anna Karenina tells of a woman who, by leaving her husband in order to live with another man, becomes an outcast from society.

▲WHO WAS MARK TWAIN?

Mark Twain was an American writer whose real name was Samuel Langhorne Clemens. He lived from 1835 to 1910, and his best-known books are *The Adventures of Tom Sawyer* and *The Adventures of Huckleberry Finn* – both written as children's stories.

Mark Twain was brought up close to the great Mississippi River, which he loved – and from which he got his pen-name. 'Mark Twain', which means 'Mark Two', was the term that indicated water that was only just deep enough for navigation.

Mark Twain's childhood was spent mainly in the town of Hannibal, Missouri, where his father kept a grocery, practised law and was active in local politics. The town was a fascinating place, where ordinary people mixed with the pilots of steamboats and wandering gamblers.

The countryside around the town was a source of adventure for the young Mark Twain. But his father died when he was only 12 years old, and he was forced to start work to help support his family. For a while he worked as a printer on a local paper (which his brother owned).

At the age of 18 he began to travel, working in various places as a printer or a journalist. At one time he worked as a river-boat pilot (he had set off for South America, but was persuaded instead to learn to navigate). Another time he prospected for gold.

Working for a Californian newspaper, he became a travel writer and visited Hawaii, the Sandwich Islands, Europe and the Holy Land. After this last trip he wrote a book about his experiences – *The Innocents Abroad*.

The Adventures of Tom Sawyer was even more popular than his earlier work. It was a story for boys, based on his own childhood experiences. *Huckleberry Finn*, which was published in 1885, and is usually considered his best work (and an important work in the history of American literature), was given the same setting. The character of Huckleberry Finn was based on a childhood friend, the son of a local drunkard.

▲ WHO WAS EMILE ZOLA?

Emile Zola was a French writer whose realistic (and often rather grim) novels set out to study life among ordinary people in the changing world of the Industrial Revolution.

Zola was born in 1840. As a young man he worked in the publishing house, Hachette.

Eventually he became a full-time writer, and published his first novel, *Thérèse Raquin*, in 1867. Next he wrote a series of novels about two families, the Rougons and the Macquarts, and the problems of alcoholism. The first of these, *The Drunkard*, was a best-seller. Other important novels in this series are *Germinal*, about a coal-mining community, and *Nana*, about a corrupt and beautiful young actress. (The picture shows her in the part of a nymph.)

Zola was a champion of liberty and in 1898 he was arrested for libel after writing an open letter in defence of a Jewish army officer, Dreyfus, on trial for treason.

He was exiled for a while in England and died in 1902.

▲ WHO WAS FRANZ KAFKA?

Franz Kafka was a writer in German, though he was born in Prague in Czechoslovakia and spent most of his life there. His best known works are two novels – *The Castle* and *The Trial*, and a short story, *Metamorphosis*.

Kafka was born in 1883. His family was Jewish (his sisters died in concentration camps in World War II) and, although he was an atheist, he was deeply interested in the Jewish religion.

He led a very quiet life, working in an insurance office and writing. He was an anxious and lonely man, and this is reflected in his books, which are often about people who seem to suffer in a cold and unsympathetic world for no clear reason.

Although Kafka was quiet he was interested in the world around him, and was a committed socialist. In 1917 he developed tuberculosis and had to spend much of his life from that time in a sanatorium. He died in 1924. The picture shows a scene from a film of *The Trial*.

▼ DID SHERLOCK HOLMES REALLY EXIST?

Sherlock Holmes must be one of the most famous detectives of all time – but the truth is that he was not a real person at all. He was the creation of the novelist Sir Arthur Conan Doyle, who lived from 1859 to 1930.

Sherlock Holmes was not the first fictional detective (Edgar Allen Poe had already created M.Dupin). But he was the first to catch the public imagination, and his character and lifestyle were so well described that many people have believed he was real and have looked for his house – which does not exist – at 221 B Baker Street, London.

The stories, mostly set in London at the end of the 19th century, include the famous tale of *The Hound of the Baskervilles*. Holmes is described as an eccentric person, with amazing powers of concentration, who smokes a pipe and plays a violin. He is helped by Dr Watson, who is rather dim and whose own slowness shows up Holmes's brilliance.

▲ WHO WAS PHIDEAS?

Phideas was a sculptor in Ancient Greece. Although almost nothing of his work survives today, his fame has lasted until modern times.

In his own day, people said that Phideas had seen the gods and through him, ordinary people could glimpse them.

It is thought that Phideas lived from about 490 to 430 BC. The ruler of Athens, Pericles, put him in charge of an important building programme which included the sculptures of the Parthenon. Phideas made a huge gold and ivory statue of the goddess Athena which, at about 10 metres tall, was the largest statue ever erected in Athens.

A later, bronze statue of Athena was even taller – but because he put his own portrait as well as Pericles's on her shield, he was accused of irreverence and sent into exile.

He also made an ivory and gold Zeus at Olympia (where the remains of Phideas's workshop have been found) and possibly some of the surviving marbles from the Parthenon.

▲ WHO WAS GIOTTO?

Giotto was an Italian artist of the early part of the era we call the Renaissance. He was the most important painter of his time, and was one of the first painters to present lifelike people in realistic backgrounds.

Giotto lived from 1266 to 1337. Like other artists of his time, he did much of his work as frescoes on chapel walls.

Among his most famous pictures are a series of frescoes in Padua, showing the life of Christ. The characters look very lifelike – something quite new in Giotto's day.

He lived and worked in many parts of Italy, at one time in Florence, and then as court painter for the ruler of Naples. By 1334 he was back in Florence as overseer of works for the cathedral and fortifications that were being built.

Giotto was the first in a long line of Italian painters to use a realistic style – although other painters of his own day continued to use a traditional style. The picture is the *Madonna in Maestà*.

▲ WHO WAS PIERO DELLA FRANCESCA?

Piero della Francesca was one of the most important artists of the Italian Renaissance. He is best known for his clear, lifelike pictures, though in his own day he was more famous for his scientific work and he did not have much influence on other painters of his time.

He was born in 1420, and died in 1492. Like other Renaissance artists, he had wide interests.

He was especially concerned with geometry, which he used to help him work out the basic patterns for his pictures and get the perspective right.

His work was often in the form of frescoes, and among the best known of these are those showing the Legend of the Holy Cross in the church of St Francis at Arrezo. Here he shows both ordinary people – peasants sitting at the feet of St Francis – and magnificent figures, such as the Queen of Sheba.

The picture shows part of an altarpiece, *The Baptism of Christ*.

◀ WHO MADE THE FIRST OIL PAINTINGS?

Strictly speaking, we do not know who made the first oil paintings, since the technique goes back to the Middle Ages. But we do know that the Flemish painters Hubert and Jan van Eyck were the first to make the most of the possibilities the method offers in terms of depth and shades of colour.

We know little of Hubert's work, but much more of Jan's, since he left many signed and dated pictures. Because Hubert died first, in 1426, people tend to think he was the elder brother.

Among Jan van Eyck's early works is a painting of the Virgin Mary in a church.

Perhaps his most famous picture is of a man named Arnolfini and his wife, at their wedding. Another – of a man in a red turban – may have been a self-portrait. We are not sure exactly what new method the van Eycks brought to oil painting, but they were famous in their own time for using an entirely new technique.

▶ WHO WAS MICHELANGELO?

Michelangelo is often said to be one of the greatest artists Europe has ever produced. He was certainly one of the most important figures in the Italian Renaissance. His best known work includes some magnificent sculpture as well as the frescoes that cover the ceiling and part of the walls of the Sistine Chapel, in the Vatican in Rome.

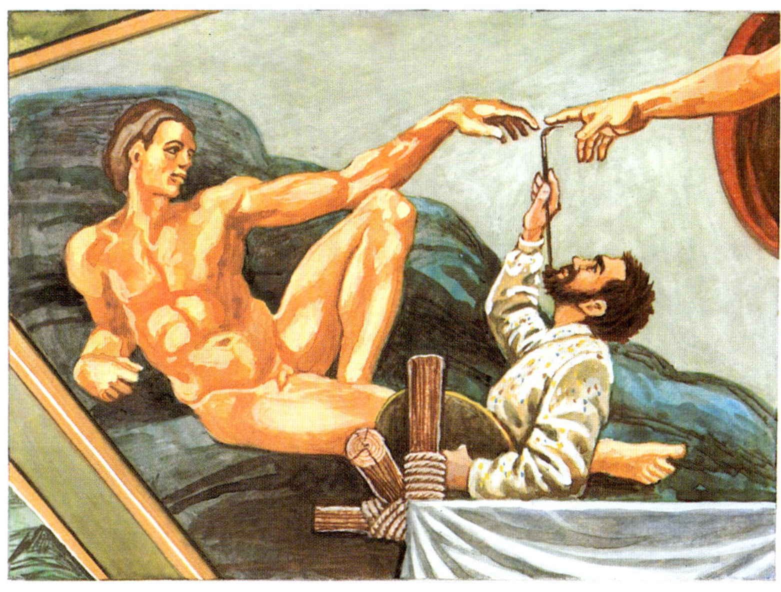

His full name was Michelangelo Buonarroti. He was born in 1475 into an aristocratic family. At first his parents tried to stop him from becoming an artist because they did not think it was a suitable profession for someone of his class, but eventually he managed to overcome their opposition. He attended a school for artists run by Bertoldo di Giovanni in the Medici Gardens in Florence.

Following a period in Bologna, Michelangelo went to Rome in 1496, where he produced one of his greatest works – his famous *Pietà*, a statue of the Virgin Mary, still looking like a young girl, with the body of the dead Christ in her arms.

Following this he returned to Florence, where he produced another masterpiece – his statue of the young Biblical king, David.

In 1505 the then Pope, Julius II, asked him to return to Rome to make a tomb. Michelangelo never managed to finish this – he quarrelled with the Pope and went back to Florence. But by 1508 he was in Rome again, painting the frescoes in the Sistine Chapel. When this work was finished, it covered the whole of the vault and part of the upper walls.

He wanted assistants to help him, but it was hard to find anyone good enough. In the end, he did almost all of it by himself in an extraordinarily short time.

Having started the mammoth task in 1508, he completed it by 1512. Many other great works followed, before Michelangelo died in 1564.

▶WHO WAS BERNINI?

Gianlorenzo Bernini was one of the most important sculptors of 17th century Italy. His style was the very ornate fashion which we now call 'Baroque'. Much of his work was done for the great church of St Peter, in the Vatican, Rome.

Bernini was born in 1598. His father – also known as Bernini – was himself a famous sculptor, which meant that from an early age the young Bernini was able to meet the famous and influential people who could find him work.

In 1639 he became the most important artist in the court of Pope Urban VIII, as well as chief architect of St Peter's. Unfortunately he had to leave this work when the Pope died as his successor, Pope Innocent X did not like his style. However, the next Pope, Alexander VII gave him back his job.

Bernini's work was not confined to sacred places. His most famous sculpture (shown in the picture) is the Fountain of the Four Rivers in the Piazza Navona in Rome. The story goes that he had to compete for this job with his arch rival, Francesco Borromini.

It is said that Bernini secured the commission by underhand means – he gave a silver model of the design to the Pope's sister-in-law. The legend goes on to say that Bernini managed to insult Borromini's own work in his design of the fountain. He shows the Nile river god shielding his eyes so that he does not have to look at the church opposite (which Borromini designed) and another god, representing the River Plate, appears so sure that the church is unstable that he has his hands raised to protect himself from falling masonry! In fact, the church was built after the fountain, so this part of the story cannot be true.

By the end of his life, Bernini's rich, ornate work could be seen in many chapels and churches throughout Rome.

He died in 1680.

◀WHO WAS RODIN?

Auguste Rodin was a French sculptor whose work, often large figures cast in bronze, includes such well-known pieces as *The Thinker* and *The Kiss*.

Rodin was born in Paris in 1840. He studied under various sculptors and worked for a while as a mason.

A trip to Italy in 1875 introduced him to the work of Michelangelo, which impressed him deeply. In 1878 he held an exhibition of his work in which his figures were so lifelike that he was accused of casting them from live models.

He was always a controversial artist – his statue of Balzac, for example, was rejected by the organisation that commissioned it because of the way it was dressed. The forceful bronze in the picture is called *The Hand of God*.

Rodin especially enjoyed the idea of conveying a feeling of movement in his work – many of his models were dancers. He died in 1917, leaving much of his work to his nation.

▲WHO WERE KNOWN AS THE POST-IMPRESSIONISTS?

The Post-Impressionists is the name given to the group of artists, working mainly in France, whose work followed the Impressionist movement of the 19th century. The name, given to the work of Seurat, Gauguin, Van Gogh and Cézanne, comes from the title of an exhibition held in London in 1910 and called *Manet and the Post-Impressionists*.

Although these artist have been grouped together by the name Post-Impressionist, their work is very different. Seurat painted very static scenes of town and suburban life, using dots and dabs of pure colour, while Gauguin chose to paint in the strong, bright, flat colours, which he associated with the South Sea islands where he lived for many years.

Van Gogh was Dutch, but worked mostly in the south of France. The picture shows part of Cézanne's *Landscape with Poplars*. His work had a strong influence on later artists, including Picasso.

▲WHO WERE KNOWN AS THE WILD BEASTS?

The group of artists known as *Les Fauves* (The Wild Beasts) worked in France at the beginning of the 20th century. They included Henri Matisse and André Derain and several other artists.

The group got its name from a critic named Louis Vauxelles who, on seeing their work on the walls of the gallery where they were exhibiting, pointed to a sculpture in the middle of the room and exclaimed: 'Donatello among the wild beasts!' In fact he was referring to the behaviour of the artists rather than their work.

But although they exhibited together (this was in 1905) they were not a definite movement in painting in the way that the Impressionists and Post-Impressionists were.

Nevertheless, they did important work, and influenced many painters who came after them. Collectively their work was the beginning of modern abstract art.

Part of Matisse's *Algerian Woman* is shown in the picture.

▲WHO WAS PICASSO?

Pablo Ruiz y Picasso was a Spanish artist who must be the best known of all 20th century painters. Throughout his long life he painted in several different styles, and greatly influenced other painters of his day.

Picasso was born in 1881 in Malaga, Spain. When he started work, the great painters of the Impressionist movement were still alive. His early pictures – done mainly in blue – showed the poverty he saw around him in Barcelona.

Later he moved to Paris where he worked with Georges Braque on pictures showing figures as fragments of geometric shapes – the style we know as cubism.

He became more deeply involved with politics, especially during the Spanish Civil War. One of Picasso's most famous pictures is *Guernica*, which depicts the destruction of a Spanish town. His work was suppressed by the Nazis in World War II.

Picasso died in the south of France in 1973.

◀FOR WHOM DID VIVALDI COMPOSE HIS MUSIC?

Antonio Vivaldi, the Italian composer who lived from 1678 to 1741, composed most of his music for the pupils of a girls' orphanage in Venice.

The orphanage was the Conservatorio della Pietà (known as the Pietà). His job was to teach the violin, but because the choir and orchestra were so good, he composed music for them.

When Vivaldi started work in 1703, he was on good terms with the governors of the Pietà, but in 1713 he upset them by taking time off work to travel about Italy, writing and producing operas.

Eventually he left his job, though he did go on composing for the Pietà. His most famous work includes the four *Four Seasons* concertos – but he wrote hundreds of other pieces. Many of these were written rather fast to fulfil his contract with the Pietà, and critics have accused him – rather unfairly – of having written the same concerto 400 times!

◀WHO WAS JOHANN SEBASTIAN BACH?

Johann Sebastian Bach was the most famous member of a family of musicians from the German town of Eisenach.

Bach was born in 1685. He was taught music first by his father, who was a professional musician, and then, when his father died, by his brother Johann Christoph.

After working for a while as an organist, Bach became musical director to a prince – Leopold of Kothen – in 1717. During this time, he composed some of his most famous work – the *Brandenburg Concertos*.

Because he was trained as a church organist, and continued to work as one, Bach inevitably wrote a lot of church music. His music for church choirs includes 200 cantatas, as well as a *Mass in B Minor*. He also wrote three settings of the Passion story, the most famous of which is his St Matthew Passion.

Bach suffered a tragedy when, in 1747, he lost his sight. He died very soon afterwards, in 1750.

▶WHO WAS MOZART?

Wolfgang Amadeus Mozart lived only 35 years, but in that time he became one of the world's most famous composers.

Mozart was born in Salzburg, in Austria in 1756. He began composing at the age of five and could play the harpsichord and violin so well that even as a very young child his father took him on a tour of Europe, playing before royalty.

As a young man, Mozart settled in Vienna, but in spite of being so talented he was always in financial difficulties.

Mozart's work included many concertos for a variety of instruments, including the piano, horn and bassoon. He also wrote symphonies and several great operas, including *The Marriage of Figaro*, *The Magic Flute*, *Don Giovanni* and *Cosi fan tutte*.

He died very suddenly after a short illness. Rumour had it that he had been poisoned, but it is more likely that he had a weak heart. He died so poor that only the gravedigger attended his funeral.

▶ WHO WAS BEETHOVEN?

Ludwig van Beethoven has been called the greatest composer who has ever lived – yet he was deaf for much of his life.

Beethoven lived from 1770 to 1827. He was born in Bonn in Germany. He was not a child prodigy, but at the age of 17 he was good enough to go to Vienna to study under Mozart.

Later, he studied with Josef Haydn, but we know he was not satisfied and took extra lessons in secret!

By the age of 32, he knew he was going deaf. Deeply depressed, he had to give up playing, but was able to go on composing because he could still hear the sound of the music in his head. He used to go for long walks, carrying a sketch book in which he wrote down his musical ideas.

He is remembered for many great works – including masterpieces such as the *Moonlight Sonata*, the *Emperor Concerto* and his famous Ninth Symphony, in which he introduced choral music for the first time in a symphony.

▶ WHO WAS TCHAIKOVSKY?

The Russian composer Peter Ilich Tchaikovsky is probably best known as the composer of ballet music, though he wrote many other pieces.

Tchaikovsky was born in 1840 in Votkinsk in Russia. He entered the St Petersburg (now Leningrad) Conservatory of Music in 1862 and from 1865 worked at the Moscow Conservatory. At first his work was unpopular.

In 1877 Tchaikovsky made a disastrous marriage which only lasted a few weeks and left him extremely depressed. In the same year, however, he was offered an income from a wealthy widow, Nadezhda von Meck, who gave him an allowance on condition that they never met! It was at this point that he began to compose most of his major works.

Tchaikovsky's most popular compositions include the ballets *Sleeping Beauty* and *Swan Lake*, the *Romeo and Juliet* Overture, the opera *Eugene Onegin* and his Sixth (*Pathétique*) Symphony.

He died of cholera in 1893.

◀ WHO WAS STRAVINSKY?

Igor Stravinsky was a Russian composer who is best known for the dramatic ballet music he wrote for the impressario Diaghilev.

Stravinsky was born in 1882 in a town in Russia then named Oranienbaum – now Lomonosov. In 1909 he spent a season working in Paris with Diaghilev and his company, the *Ballets Russes*. Stravinsky wrote several scores for the ballet, including *The Firebird* (shown in the picture), *Petrushka* (a ballet based on a story of rivalry among the characters in a puppet show) and *The Rite of Spring*.

The last composition was very controversial. The first audience that heard it made so much noise that the music could hardly be heard! But today it is recognised as one of Stravinsky's best works.

During World War I, Stravinsky and his family lived in Switzerland. At the outbreak of World War II he emigrated to the United States where he lived and worked until his death in 1971.

▼WHO COMBINED FOLK MUSIC WITH BACH?

The Brazilian composer Heitor Villa-Lobos is especially famous for having combined the traditional folk music of his own country with the style and approach of the much earlier composer, J S Bach.

Villa-Lobos was born in 1887. As a young man he travelled around Brazil and learned as much as he could about his country's folk music. He also studied classical music at Brazil's Instituto Nacional de Musica. His first compositions were published in 1915.

In 1919 he was lucky enough to meet the famous concert pianist Artur Rubenstein, who made Villa-Lobos's work popular by playing it in many parts of the world.

The works in which he combined the method of Bach with folk music include a collection of nine pieces for various instruments, which he called *Bachianos Brasilieras*, and another collection of 14 works called the *Choros*. Villa-Lobos died in 1959.

▲WHO MADE THE GUITAR A CONCERT INSTRUMENT?

The guitar is a traditional instrument which until the 20th century was used mainly to play the folk music of Spain. Today it is a concert instrument as well – a development that is almost entirely the result of the work of the guitarist Andres Segovia.

Segovia was born in Spain in 1894. Because his parents did not want him to have a musical career, they did not help him and he was largely self-taught. He did go to college though – to the Granada Musical Institute.

In 1910, while he was a student there, he gave his first public concert. Later concerts outside Spain helped him to break away from folk guitar playing and he became interested in the idea of arranging classical music for the guitar.

He began with lute music, and then went on to make arrangements of music by many composers, including J S Bach, Handel, Mozart and Brahms.

▼WHICH OPERA SINGER WAS ONE OF THE FIRST RECORDING STARS?

Many great singers from the past live on in name only. But one opera singer can still be heard today even though he died as long ago as 1921. This is Enrico Caruso, an Italian tenor who was the first opera singer to achieve worldwide fame through recordings.

Caruso was born in Naples in 1873. He became famous after singing at La Scala Opera House in Milan in 1898, in the part of Rudolfo in Puccini's *La Bohème*. From then on he sang many tenor parts in the great opera houses of the world.

But his audience was far greater than that. For in 1902 Caruso began to make recordings, using what was then known as the phonograph. He continued to make records until, in 1920, he was taken ill while he was singing. Pneumonia was diagnosed and he died soon afterwards. A film about his life – *The Great Caruso*, starring Mario Lanza – was made in 1950.

▼WHO WAS 'DUKE' ELLINGTON?

Edward Kennedy Ellington – known throughout most of his life as 'Duke' Ellington – was a famous American jazz musician and band leader who had considerable influence on popular music in the 20th century.

Duke Ellington was born in Washington DC in 1899. After working briefly running a small sign-writing business, he took up music full-time. His musical career as the leader of an orchestra and a brilliant solo pianist lasted for 55 years. During that time he and his orchestra played in a huge number of concerts, made records and worked with great singers such as Ella Fitzgerald and Billie Holiday.

It was during a series of annual concerts at Carnegie Hall between 1945 and 1950 that he first played one of his most famous compositions, *Black Brown and Beige*.

As well as composing music, he made arrangements of both popular and classical music.

Duke Ellington died in 1974.

▲WHO WAS BILLIE HOLIDAY?

Billie Holiday is remembered not only as the most moving jazz singer of her day – but also as a tragic person whose unhappy life was reflected in the bitter-sweet songs she sang and her style of singing.

She was born in Baltimore, Maryland in 1915. Her parents were very young and unmarried – her early life was hard and she had to fend for herself from the age of 12.

In 1929 she moved to New York with her mother, and began to sing in Harlem clubs. Although she was very young, she had a mature voice and soon began to meet with success. She performed for some of the greatest jazz band leaders of her day – including Duke Ellington, Benny Goodman and Count Basie.

The hardships she suffered when she was young left her a deeply unhappy person, and she turned to alcohol and then drugs to help her. But these damaged her voice and eventually led to her death as a heroin addict in 1959.

▼WHO WAS MARIA CALLAS?

Maria Callas was an American-born, Greek opera singer, with an unusual voice, fine acting ability and a fiery personality.

Maria Callas was born Maria Kalogeropoulou, in New York City in 1923. The family went home to Greece when she was 13, and she won a scholarship to the Royal Conservatory in Athens soon afterwards. She made her stage debut in Athens when she was only 14, singing in Mascagni's *Cavalleria Rusticana*.

She sang at the great La Scala opera house in Milan between 1951 and 1958 – and was soon an international star, performing at the most famous opera houses in the world.

Many critics think she sang best in Italian opera – her most famous roles were in *La Traviata*, *Tosca*, *Lucia di Lammermoor* and as the enchantress of Greek myth, *Medea*. Later, she played the part of Medea for the Italian film-maker Pasolini.

Maria Callas died in 1977.

◀WHO WROTE THE FIRST TRAGEDIES?

Tragedy is a kind of drama that grew up in Ancient Greece. Among the early writers of tragedy, the best-known are Aeschylus, Sophocles and Euripides.

Aeschylus lived from 525 to 456 BC. Only seven of his 90 plays survive – we do not, for example, have the first play for which he won a prize in 484 BC. He wrote a new kind of play – using two actors. Until that time, there had been just one actor and a chorus.

Sophocles (496-406 BC) brought in more changes – a third speaker, a less important part for the chorus and a new kind of trilogy (group of three plays) in which each play was complete in itself. We still have seven – including his most famous, *Oedipus Rex*.

Euripides (484-406 BC) was the last of the three. His plays are despairing and often violent, but in later life he started writing tragi-comedies with happy endings. This started a new trend in Greek drama.

◀WHO ARE COLUMBINE AND HARLEQUIN?

Columbine and Harlequin are two main characters in the *Commedia dell'arte* – a form of traditional theatre that started in Italy at the end of the Renaissance and which was popular all over Europe until the 18th century.

Commedia dell'arte was based on very simple plots – usually involving young lovers whose parents do not want them to marry, and a group of witty and intelligent servants, who help them. Each character had a special mask and costume. Into this action, entertainment such as acrobatics, juggling and music were added. The characters of Harlequin and Columbine developed from the French form of this theatre.

Originally they were Arlecchino and Columbina – two of the servants who help the lovers. Arlecchino was at first dressed in rags, but over the years his costume developed into the one we know today. Columbina was shown as a young girl – often loved by Arlecchino.

◀WHO WAS ENGLAND'S GREATEST DRAMATIST?

England's greatest dramatist was also one of the world's greatest – William Shakespeare, the author of 35 plays, whose work remains the most important drama ever written in English.

Shakespeare was born in 1564, in Stratford-on-Avon in Warwickshire. He was educated there and married, but eventually left and went to London, where he became involved with the theatre. He joined a company named the Chamberlain's Men, later called The King's Men, based at the Globe Theatre.

Here he became an actor and a director, writing plays for the company to perform, and probably producing them too. His plays cover a wide variety of subject matter and include histories, light comedies such as *A Midsummer Night's Dream* (left) and dark tragedies such as *Hamlet* and *King Lear*.

As well as writing plays, he was also a poet, and published a collection of sonnets in 1609. He died in 1616.

▶WHO WAS MOLIÈRE?

Molière – whose real name was Jean-Baptiste Poquelin – was a French writer and great comic dramatist. Among his best known works are *Tartuffe*, *Le Misanthrope* and *Le Bourgeois Gentilhomme*.

Molière was born in 1622 in Paris. As a young man, he set up a theatrical company financed in part by an actress, Madeleine Béjart. The company was not an immediate success and Molière ended up in jail twice for debt.

But eventually things did begin to go well and, in 1658, they played before the King.

Molière became well-known as a playwright – but his work often offended the church. One of his best known works is *Tartuffe*, about a hypocritical religious man who is eventually unmasked. This was banned for five years, but when it was eventually shown, it was a great success.

Molière was a brilliant comic actor, and took part in his own plays. In 1673 he was taken ill while actually on stage, and taken home to die.

▶WHO SOLD HIS SOUL TO THE DEVIL?

There is a German legend, dating back to the 16th century, about a magician named Faust who sold his soul to the devil in return for knowledge and power. The story has been written many times, but one of the most important versions of it is a dramatic poem by the German writer, Johann Wolfgang von Goethe.

Goethe was born in 1749. As well as being a playwright, he was a critic, journalist, theatre manager, painter, poet and scientist.

His version of the Faust legend was published in two parts – the first in 1808, the second in 1832, the year of his death. He tackled the story in a different way from earlier versions (such as that by the English playwright, Christopher Marlowe) since he saves Faust instead of sending him to hell.

Goethe – a brilliant scholar himself – could not accept that a thirst for knowledge could lead to damnation.

▶WHO WAS KNOWN AS 'THE DIVINE SARAH'?

'The Divine Sarah' was the name critics gave to the great French actress Sarah Bernhardt.

Sarah Bernhardt, born Henriette Bernard in 1844, spent much of her childhood in a convent and had almost decided to become a nun, but instead one of her mother's friends persuaded her to take up acting.

After finishing training, she slowly built up her reputation until, after a very successful tour in London with France's national theatre company, the *Comédie Francaise*, she set up her own company in 1880.

She became particularly famous for her role as Marguerite Gautier, the heroine of *La Dame aux Camelias*, by Dumas.

In 1905, she injured her knee, and over the next ten years it grew gradually worse until she had the leg amputated. But she continued to act in any part she could do seated. She died in 1923.

◀WHO WAS ANTON CHEKHOV?

Anton Chekhov was a Russian playwright and writer of short stories. Among his best-known works are the plays *Uncle Vanya* and *The Seagull*. His plays are often about the decline of the Russian land-owning class.

Chekhov was born in 1860 in the seaside town of Taganrog. As a young man he trained as a doctor in Moscow, and supported himself and his family by writing comic sketches for magazines. He later built up a reputation as a dramatist and short-story writer.

Eventually he was able to afford an estate south of Moscow, where he lived with his sister until he realised he had tuberculosis and would have to move to the coast for his health. He went to live in Yalta on the Black Sea, and also spent some time in France.

Two of his best-known plays – *The Cherry Orchard* and *The Three Sisters* – were written at this time.

He died in 1904.

▶WHO WAS ELEONORA DUSE?

Elenora Duse (right) was an Italian actress who was famous for the way she played leading roles in plays by the Norwegian dramatist, Henrik Ibsen.

Eleonora Duse was born in a railway carriage in Italy in 1858. Her family were involved in the theatre, and she first appeared on stage at the age of four – taking leading roles from the age of 14. She first became famous after playing the part of Thérèse Raquin, in a play based on Zola's novel.

Eleonora Duse retired in 1909 because of ill-health, and died in 1923.

Her style was quite different from that of Sarah Bernhardt, who was almost the same age. Instead of projecting her own personality she worked hard at trying to understand the character of the part she was acting. This was particularly important to her when she played in dramas by the young poet Gabriele D'Annunzio, with whom she was in love, and also in Ibsen's plays.

▲WHO WAS IBSEN?

Henrik Ibsen was a Norwegian dramatist who is known as the father of modern drama because he introduced social problems into his plays in a realistic manner.

Henrik Ibsen was born in 1828 in the sea-port of Skein. After training as a chemist, he worked first in Bergen and then in the capital of Norway, Christiana (now called Oslo), writing and directing plays. He left Norway in 1862, and stayed away for 27 years – living mainly in Rome, but also in Munich and Dresden.

These were the years in which he wrote many of his best known plays – starting with *Brand* and *Peer Gynt* and going on to *The Pillars of Society*, *Ghosts*, *The Wild Duck*, *A Doll's House* and several others which examine moral issues.

On his return to Norway near the end of his life, Ibsen wrote two of his most famous plays – *John Gabriel Borkman* and *Hedda Gabler*.

Ibsen died in 1906.

▲WHO WAS ANNA PAVLOVA?

Anna Pavlova was a great Russian ballerina who was famous for her solo performances, especially one called *The Dying Swan*.

She was born in 1882 in St Petersburg – now called Leningrad. As a child, she was lucky enough to be accepted by one of the most famous ballet schools of the time, the Imperial School of Ballet in St Petersburg. Later she joined the Mariinsky Theatre Company and became prima ballerina.

She became internationally famous in 1909, when she travelled with the impressario Diaghilev and a company made up of dancers from the Mariinsky and Bolshoi theatres – the *Ballets Russes*.

Next, she performed in London, where she was a huge success. In 1913, she decided she wanted more independence, set up her own company with her husband and ran it for the rest of her life.

She died in 1931, of pneumonia.

▲WHO WAS VASLAV NIJINSKY?

Vaslav Nijinsky was one of the greatest-ever male ballet dancers – known for his amazingly high leaps (elevation) and his extremely expressive and dramatic interpretations. He was also a great choreographer, producing controversial new ballets.

Nijinsky was born in 1890, in Kiev in the Ukraine. Both his parents were dancers.

He entered the Imperial School of Ballet in St Petersburg, where he was a star before he finished training. When he joined the Mariinsky Theatre, he partnered some of the greatest ballerinas of the day.

Like Anna Pavlova, he went to Paris in 1909 with Diaghilev's Ballets Russes. He was a resounding success.

As a choreographer he broke away from the classical style of dancing.

In 1919, after a nervous breakdown which was said to be caused by schizophrenia, he left the stage. He died in London in 1950.

▲WHO WAS BERTHOLD BRECHT?

Berthold Brecht was a German playwright who had an important influence on 20th century drama. He developed a theory of drama whereby the audience was made to criticise, instead of identifying with, the characters.

Brecht was born in Bavaria in 1898.

After his first successful play – *Baal* – his plays became more socialist. One such play was *The Threepenny Opera*, which, with its music by Kurt Weill, was a huge success.

With the rise of Hitler, Brecht was forced to leave Germany. He went first to Scandinavia and then to the United States. It was while he was there that he wrote his most famous work, *The Caucasian Chalk Circle*.

He left the United States in 1947, because of political pressure. From then, until his death in 1956, he worked mainly in East Berlin, where he had his own company, the *Berliner Ensemble*.

▶WHO WAS CHARLIE CHAPLIN?

Charlie Chaplin was one of the greatest cinema stars of all time. He made his name in the early silent films as a comic actor – famous for his costume which consisted of a bowler hat, tight jacket, baggy trousers and huge shoes.

Charles Spencer Chaplin was born in London in 1889. His family was very poor.

He first went on stage when he was still a child.

In 1913 a Hollywood film company, Keystone, signed him up and he began to appear in films. He soon became a star, playing the part of a confused little man, constantly in some sort of difficulty.

Among his best known films are *The Gold Rush* and *Modern Times*, as well as his first talking picture, *The Great Dictator*.

Chaplin left the United States in 1952 because of political pressure and lived in Switzerland for the rest of his life. He was knighted in 1975 and died in 1977.

◀WHO WERE LAUREL AND HARDY?

Laurel and Hardy were one of the most popular comedy teams ever to appear in the cinema. They made both silent and talking films between 1926 and 1952.

Stan Laurel's real name was Arthur Stanley Jefferson. He was born in 1890 in Ulverston, Lancashire, England. He began his career in music halls and went to the United States in 1910.

Oliver Norvell Hardy was born in 1893 in Georgia in the southern United States. He arrived in Hollywood in 1918.

Laurel and Hardy had both made films before they began to work together, in 1926. Their first film was *Putting the Pants on Philip*, and they went on to make 60 short films and 27 feature-length ones. Laurel played the part of a timid fool, while Hardy played a fat bully.

Among their best known films are *Sons of the Desert*, *Way Out West* and *Blockheads*.

Oliver Hardy died in 1957 and Stan Laurel in 1965.

▶WHO WAS LOUIS ARMSTRONG?

Louis 'Satchmo' Armstrong was a jazz trumpeter who became famous as a solo performer, a bandleader, singer and entertainer.

He was born in New Orleans in 1900. As a child he got to know many of the musicians in that city and as a young man he played in bands on the Mississippi river boats.

In 1922 he joined a Chicago-based jazz band led by a musician named Joe Oliver. He made several records with Oliver's *Creole Jazz Band*, but soon moved on to become a solo trumpeter playing with a small backing group.

He is said to be the inventor of 'scat' singing – singing meaningless syllables instead of words.

From the 1930s he became a bandleader, and more of an all-round entertainer. He appeared in several films, including *Diamond Lil*, with Mae West and, much later, *Hello Dolly*, with Barbra Streisand.

He died in 1971.

◄WHO CREATED MICKEY MOUSE?

The world-famous cartoon character Mickey Mouse was the creation of Walt Disney – the great pioneer of cartoon films. As well as Mickey, Disney created Donald Duck and countless others.

Disney lived from 1901 to 1966 and began making successful cartoon films in Los Angeles in the 1920s. In 1928 the first talking pictures had just been made and Disney had a huge hit with a Mickey Mouse 'talkie' *Steamboat Willie*.

Other triumphs followed, including *The Three Little Pigs* (with the song *Who's Afraid of the Big Bad Wolf?*). When colour films arrived, Disney made the first feature-length cartoon film, *Snow White and the Seven Dwarfs*.

In the 1940s he began making nature films – one of the best known being *The Living Desert*. Later still came children's films using a combination of live actors and animated cartoon characters. One of the most popular was *Mary Poppins*, made in 1964.

►WHO WAS ELVIS PRESLEY?

Elvis Presley was one of the first 'pop' stars – a rock 'n' roll singer whose appearance on stage could almost cause a riot. He was most popular in the 1950s and 1960s with songs such as *Heartbreak Hotel*, *Jailhouse Rock*, and *His Latest Flame*.

Born in 1935, Elvis came from a poor family from the deep south of America. He spent much of his early life in Memphis, Tennessee, where he made his first records.

In 1955, he was signed on by a big record company. Soon he was an international star – though not popular with everyone. He wore bright clothes, sang loudly with a strong rhythm and wiggled his hips as he sang. Many people were shocked!

Elvis's music had an enormous influence on later pop singers, such as the Beatles, but his own popularity began to grow less. He was a hypochondriac, and took large numbers of pills. These eventually killed him in 1979.

◄WHO WERE THE BEATLES?

The Beatles were a group of four rock musicians from Liverpool, who became famous in the 1960s.

The four Beatles were John Lennon (1940-1980), Paul McCartney (born 1942), George Harrison (born 1943) and Ringo Starr (whose real name was Richard Starkey – born 1940).

The group's early years, before Ringo joined them, were spent largely in Hamburg and in Liverpool. Success came in 1962, with a song called *Love Me Do*. This was followed in 1963 by a much bigger hit, *Please Please Me*.

By now world famous, the Beatles began to change their style. They were influenced by Indian music and religion, and the 'flower power' ideas of the 1960s.

After making several albums, the Beatles broke up in 1970. Paul McCartney and John Lennon had some success as solo artists. John was tragically shot dead in New York in 1980 at 40 years old.

MEDICINE

▼WHO WERE THE FIRST DOCTORS?

The beginnings of medicine go back to prehistoric times. But for thousands of years medicine was based largely on superstition.

We know very little about prehistoric medicine. But people must have learned a good deal about the human body as they treated wounds and broken bones. One prehistoric 'cure' for disease was the practice of trepanning. In this operation a surgeon cut a round piece of bone out of the patient's skull. Evil spirits were then supposed to come out of the hole.

Among the best of the ancient doctors were the Egyptians. By about 1500 BC they had developed a large vocabulary of special medical words and were experimenting in surgery and pharmacy.

▼WHO IS KNOWN AS THE FATHER OF MEDICINE?

In about 400 BC the Greek physician Hippocrates (460-c.370 BC) founded the first school of medicine on the island of Cos.

Doctors at the Hippocratic school of medicine were taught that diseases were the result of parts of the body not working properly, rather than of possession by demons. But Hippocrates and his followers did not know enough about the structure of the human body. They believed that diseases were caused by an imbalance of four vital fluids, or 'humours' – blood, bile, phlegm and black bile.

Over 50 books were written by Hippocrates and other members of the school. The medical code of practice called the Hippocratic Oath also dates from this time.

▼WHO WAS GALEN?

Galen (c.130-c.200) was one of the greatest Greek anatomists. His ideas remained popular for hundreds of years.

Galen was born in Pergamum (now in Turkey). When he was about 30 years old he became physician at the gladiatorial school there. Later he settled in Rome and began studying anatomy. He studied a number of animals but not humans.

Galen worked out an idea of how the body's physiological system worked. The body was supposed to contain spirits which ebbed and flowed through the arteries, veins and nerves. Many of Galen's ideas were wrong, as they were based on theory and old textbooks, rather than the study of human anatomy. But they remained popular until the 1500s.

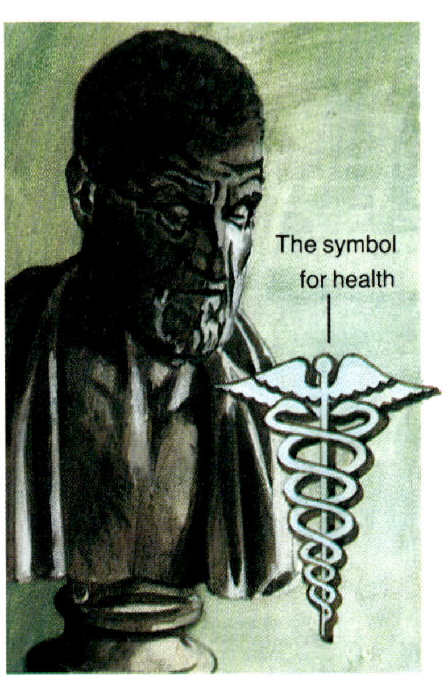

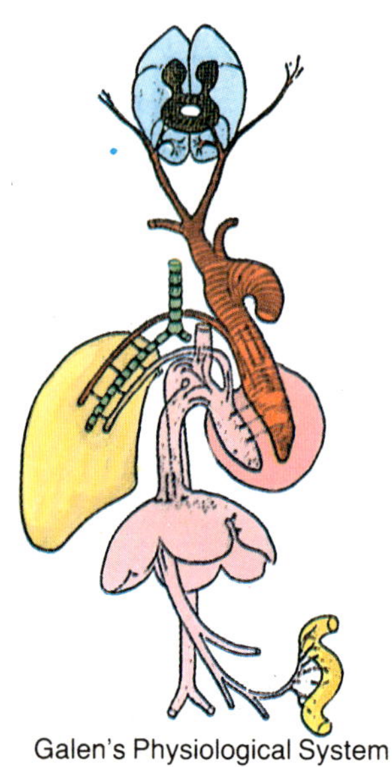

Galen's Physiological System

▼WHO FIRST PRACTISED ACUPUNCTURE?

Acupuncture – the use of needles inserted in the body – has been used in Chinese medicine for thousands of years.

In the Chinese Taoist religion order in the body depends on two opposite states called yang and yin. Yang is associated with light, the Sun, the south, masculinity and dryness. Yin is associated with darkness, the Moon, the north, femininity and wetness. All illness is thought to be an imbalance between these two states.

Acupuncture is used to restore the balance of yang and yin. The needles vary from 2 to 25 centimetres in length. They are inserted at one or more of over 800 points lying along certain lines on the human body. The needles may be left in for several hours. This form of treatment is still used today and surgery is often performed using acupuncture instead of anaesthetics.

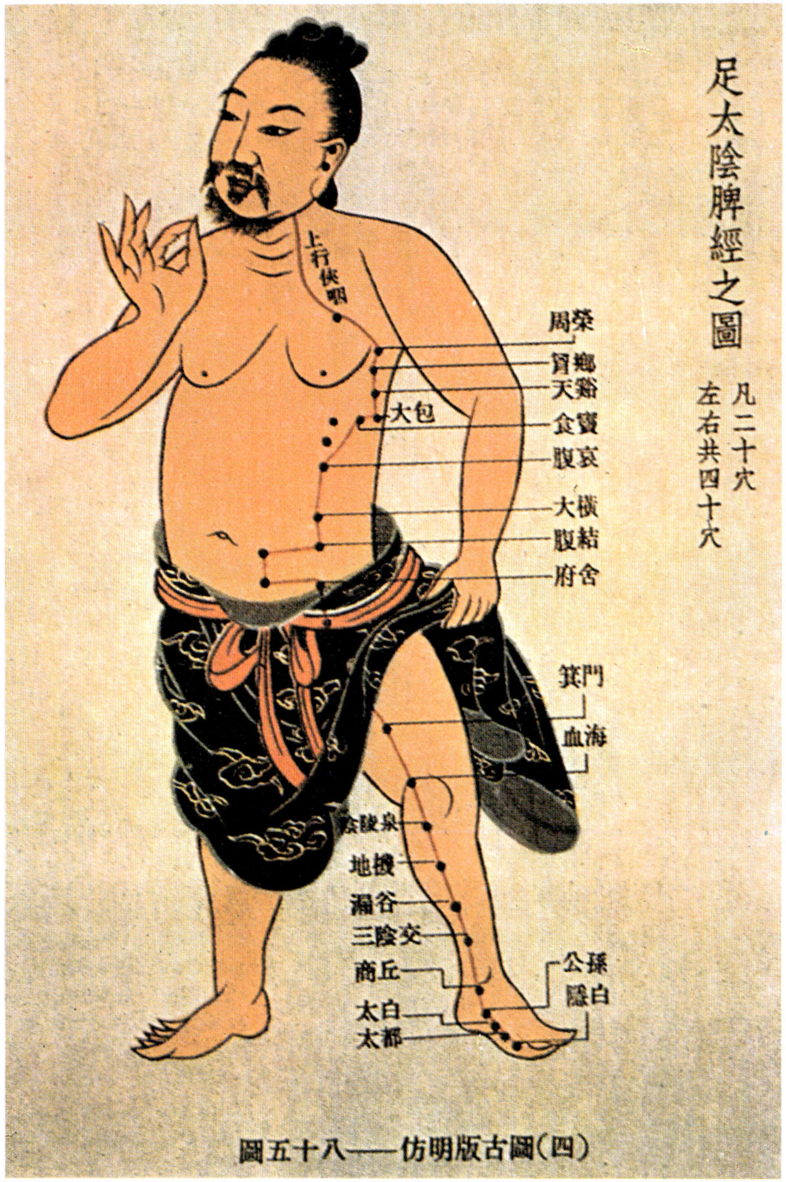

▼WHO WAS PARACELSUS?

Paracelsus (1493-1541) was a Swiss physician. His real name was Theophrastus Bombastus von Hohenheim. He was a vain man and lived up to his middle name. He took the name Paracelsus because it meant 'better than Celsus', a popular Roman physician.

Paracelsus made several important contributions to medicine. For example he wrote the first work on an occupational disease – 'Miners' sickness'. He also insisted on cleanliness as being essential for good health. He was the first to use laudanum and is sometimes called the father of anaesthesia. One of his most important ideas was that alchemists should study how to make medicines and not gold.

Paracelsus became Professor of Medicine at Basle University in 1527. Before starting his first lecture he publicly burnt books by Galen. This emphasized his idea that medicine should be studied by referring to human patients instead of just to textbooks.

▼WHO MADE THE FIRST ARTIFICIAL LIMBS?

Ambroise Paré (1510-1590) was a French surgeon. He improved the practice of surgery in several ways and devised several ingenious artificial limbs.

In the 1500s surgery was not practised by physicians. Instead it was one of the specialities of the haircutting profession. As a boy Paré started as a barber's apprentice. In 1541 he qualified as a barber-surgeon and joined the army. Eventually, he became surgeon to the French King Henry II and the King's three sons, who later succeeded him.

Paré was a popular surgeon, largely because of the improvements he introduced. For example he gave up the practice of cauterizing wounds with boiling oil. Instead he tied off the exposed arteries and covered the wounds with simple dressings.

Paré devised several artificial limbs. Among these was an arm that could be bent at the elbow and a hand with moveable fingers.

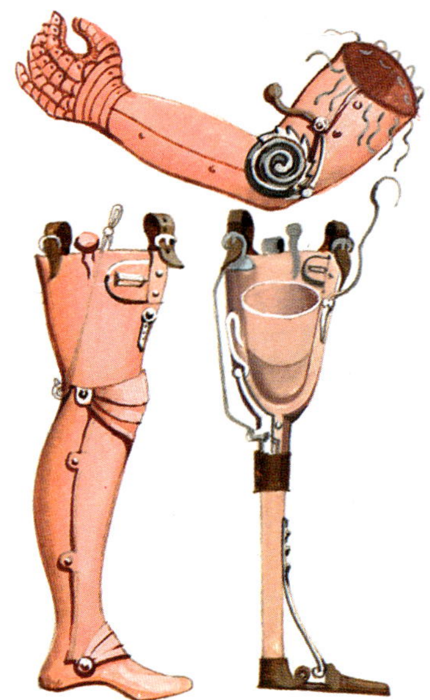

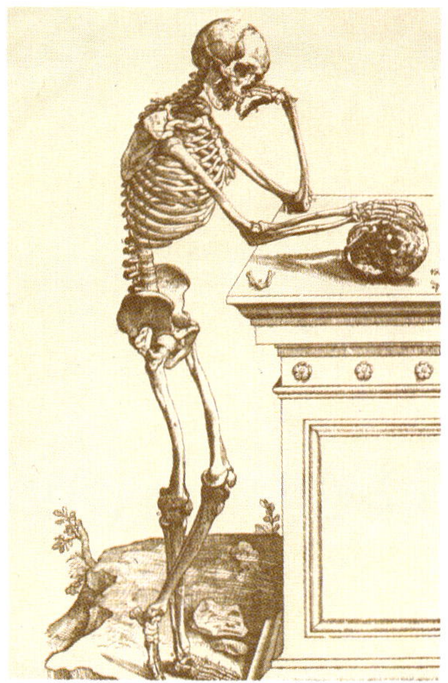

▲WHO WAS THE GREATEST EARLY ANATOMIST?

Andreas Vesalius (1514-1564), a Flemish physician, made the first really accurate studies of human anatomy.

Galen's ideas about human anatomy persisted throughout the Middle Ages. This was partly due to the fact that anatomists did not perform their own dissections.

The first to change this practice was an Italian, Mondino de Luzzi (c. 1275-1326), who wrote the first book devoted entirely to anatomy. But the study of anatomy remained much the same until the time of Vesalius.

Vesalius taught anatomy at several Italian universities. Like de Luzzi, he began to do his own dissections, mostly because he was appalled at how badly dissections were being done by anatomy assistants. After much research he wrote one of the greatest books in the history of science. It was called *De Corporis Humani Fabrica* ('On the Structure of the Human Body'). One of its illustrations is shown above.

▲WHO DISCOVERED THE CIRCULATION OF THE BLOOD?

The English doctor William Harvey (1578-1657) was the first to realize how blood passes round the body.

William Harvey spent much time doing research on the heart and blood vessels. Eventually, he came to the conclusion that Galen was wrong. Blood did not ebb and flow. It flowed through the heart, veins and arteries in one direction only. One-way valves in the heart and veins prevented it from flowing in the opposite direction.

Harvey's theory relied on the fact that there had to be a connection between the arteries and veins. Harvey decided that, as both veins and arteries divided into smaller and smaller branches, the connecting vessels must be too small for the eye to see. Italian physiologist Marcello Malpighi (1628-1694) later proved this with the aid of a microscope.

Harvey published his ideas in 1628. At first they were ridiculed, but before he died they had become accepted.

▲WHO DISCOVERED A CURE FOR SCURVY?

The Scottish doctor James Lind (1716-1794) discovered in 1747 that eating fruit prevented scurvy.

Lind realized that scurvy only appeared when people's diet was short of fresh fruit and vegetables. He managed to convince Captain Cook, who successfully prevented scurvy onboard his ships in the 1770s. Finally, in 1795 the British Navy began to issue lime juice to sailors.

▲WHO DISCOVERED THAT GERMS CAUSE DISEASE?

In 1866 the French chemist Louis Pasteur (1822-1895) was the first to realize that diseases are caused by tiny organisms, or germs. But this was only one of the great scientist's achievements.

Louis Pasteur was not a biologist or a physician but a chemist.

In 1854 he decided to work on the fermentation of wine and beer, showing that a living organism – yeast – was involved. To prevent wine going sour as it aged, he introduced the idea of heating it to 120°F (49°C) to kill off the unwanted yeast cells. This technique became known as 'pasteurization', which is still used to kill germs in milk.

In 1860 Pasteur finally disproved the idea that living micro-organisms could be generated out of nothing, through the decomposition of substances. He showed that the air contains spores of already existing micro-organisms (germs), which can infect food and other materials. In 1865 he helped to save the French silk industry by detecting a tiny parasite that was attacking the silkworms and their food.

All this work eventually led Pasteur to believe that germs were the cause of disease and that they could be spread from one person to another.

In 1881 Pasteur successfully tried out a vaccine for anthrax, a fatal disease of cattle and sheep. In 1885 he managed to prevent a case of rabies. The Pasteur Institute, established in 1888 to treat rabies, is now one of the world's most famous centres of biological research.

►WHO INTRODUCED VACCINATION AGAINST SMALLPOX?

In 1796 the English doctor Edward Jenner (1749-1827) discovered that a person inoculated with cowpox could not get smallpox.

Smallpox was once one of the world's most dreaded diseases. In the 1700s one in three of those who caught it died.

However, Jenner noticed that those who got the disease mildly never caught it again. He began to think about inoculation – but with what? At the time it was believed by country people that those who caught the mild disease cowpox never got smallpox. Jenner decided to test this. In 1786 he found a milkmaid with cowpox. He took fluid from one of her blisters and injected it into a boy. A few days later he inoculated the boy with smallpox germs. The boy didn't develop the disease.

Within a few years the practice of vaccination against smallpox became common and it has now been completely wiped out.

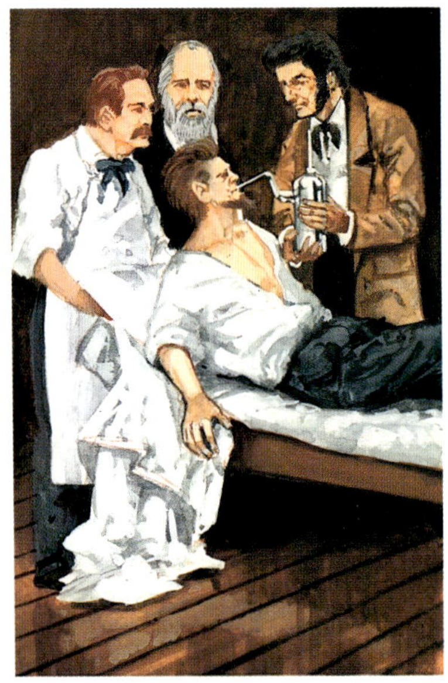

Lister's carbolic spray

▲WHO INTRODUCED THE USE OF ANAESTHETICS?

An American dentist called William Morton (1819-1868) was the first to publicize the idea of using anaesthetics in surgery.

William Morton was not the discoverer of anaesthetics. In 1800 Humphry Davy (1778-1829) had discovered laughing gas, or nitrous oxide. In 1831 chloroform was discovered by the American chemist Samuel Guthrie (1782-1848). And the term 'anaesthetic' was first suggested by an American doctor called Oliver Wendell Holmes (1809-1894).

The first recorded use of an anaesthetic in surgery was in 1842. Crawford Long (1815-1878), another American doctor, used ether to remove a neck tumour.

In 1844 William Morton, looking for a painless way to extract teeth, began taking an interest in ether. Together with an American chemist called Charles Jackson (1805-80), he patented a process for producing anaesthesia. His first operation using ether took place in September 1846.

▲WHO FIRST USED ANTISEPTICS IN SURGERY?

In 1865 the English surgeon Joseph Lister (1827-1912) used carbolic acid to prevent infection.

Joseph Lister qualified as a doctor in 1852. He became a surgeon and his particular interest was in amputation (removing limbs). The technique of anaesthesia had recently been introduced by William Morton and Lister was pleased that he could now perform painless operations. However, the fact that many patients died later from infection worried him.

In 1865 he learned of Pasteur's work on germs and diseases and began trying to kill germs in surgical wounds. He experimented with various chemicals and eventually found that dressings soaked in carbolic acid were effective. The first patient to be successfully treated in this way was a five-year-old boy with a fractured shin. Lister also used a carbolic spray to create an antiseptic mist round the operating table. But this was later found to be unnecessary.

▲WHO IDENTIFIED THE BACTERIUM THAT CAUSES TUBERCULOSIS?

The German scientist Robert Koch (1843-1910) discovered the tubercle bacillus in 1883. For this work he was awarded the Nobel Prize for Medicine and Physiology in 1905.

Robert Koch began studying disease while still a country doctor living near Breslau. He looked particularly at the bacterium that causes anthrax in cattle, and succeeded in cultivating the bacterium in blood serum and studying its whole life-cycle.

Koch then moved to Berlin and, as his fame grew, developed important techniques for the study of bacteria. Among these was the now standard method of growing bacteria on agar-agar jelly. He also established rules for identifying the bacteria that cause particular diseases.

Among the many bacteria that Koch discovered, the most important were those that cause tuberculosis, cholera and bubonic plague. With Pasteur, Koch is regarded as the founder of medical bacteriology.

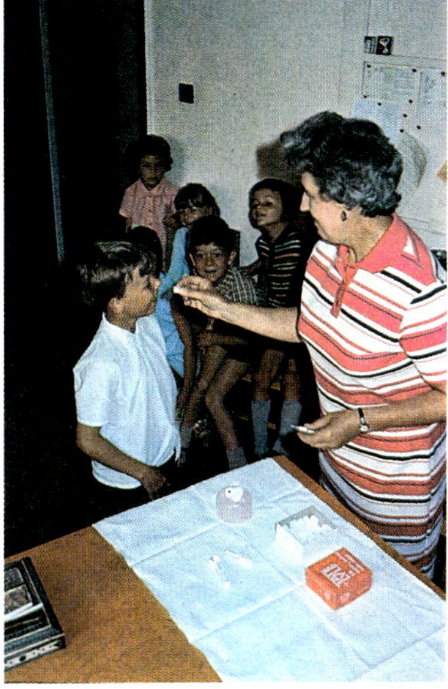

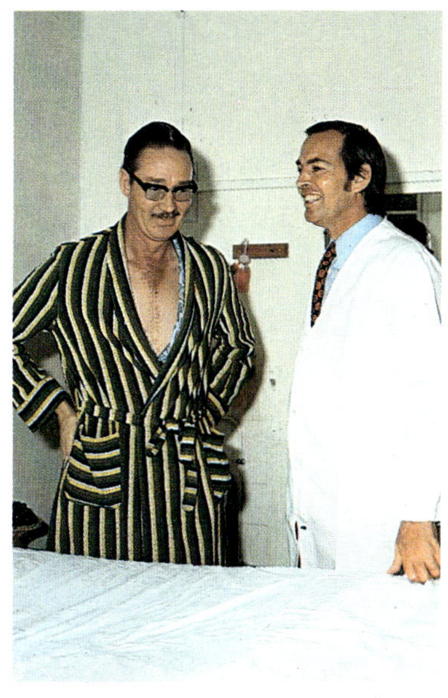

▲WHO WAS SIGMUND FREUD?

Sigmund Freud (1856-1939) was an Austrian psychiatrist. He was the founder of the technique called psychoanalysis and is famous for his ideas on dreams and child development.

After obtaining a degree in medicine in 1881 Freud studied the biology of the nervous system – in particular nerve cells. But he soon became more interested in the psychological aspect of the brain and learned that certain mental disorders could be helped by hypnosis.

Freud later abandoned hypnosis in favour of a technique he called 'free association' or the 'talking cure', in which patients were psychoanalysed by making them talk about incidents that had greatly affected them in their childhood and that they could not face up to. Freud also believed that dreams were able to show what was going on in the unconscious mind. In 1900 he published a book called *The Interpretation of Dreams*.

▲WHO FOUND A WAY OF PREVENTING POLIO?

The first vaccine that successfully prevented poliomyelitis was produced by the American microbiologist Jonas Salk (1914-).

Robert Koch and others had been very successful in cultivating bacteria. But viruses were more difficult. In 1949, however, the American microbiologist John Enders (1897-) and others succeeded in growing some polio virus.

The polio virus could now be studied easily. Salk began trying to kill the virus in a way that made it unable to cause the disease but left it able to cause the production of protective antibodies. He succeeded in 1952 and two years later the vaccine was produced in large quantities.

In 1957 another American microbiologist, Albert Sabin (1906-), produced polio vaccines that contained strains of live viruses that were too feeble to actually cause polio. Mass vaccination against polio began and by 1960 the occurrence of the disease had been greatly reduced.

▲WHO PERFORMED THE FIRST HEART TRANSPLANT?

The world's first human heart transplant was carried out on December 3 1967 by the South African surgeon Christiaan Barnard (1922-).

Surgeons began trying to transplant organs such as kidneys and hearts in the 1940s. But the main problem was that the body's natural defence system tended to 'reject' a new organ.

This problem was eventually eased by the discovery that if the tissue types of both people were carefully matched, the person receiving the heart had a much better chance of survival. At the same time it was discovered that drugs could be used to control the body's defence system which usually rejects 'foreign bodies'.

Since Barnard's first transplant hundreds of such operations have been carried out all over the world. Even babies are now receiving new hearts. However, heart transplants are very complex operations and control drugs make patients more liable to get diseases.

OUT IN SPACE

▼WHO FIRST CLAIMED THAT THE EARTH REVOLVES AROUND THE SUN?

Aristarchus lived in Alexandria from about 320-250 BC at a time when most people thought that the Earth was fixed at the centre of the universe. He disagreed, and suggested that it revolves around the Sun. It took almost 2000 years before he was proved correct.

Aristarchus also tried to measure the distance of the Moon from Earth compared with that of the Sun. His observations were made without a telescope, and his results were not very accurate – he concluded that the Sun is 20 times as far off as the Moon, while the true ratio is 400 times.

He also believed that the diameter of the Moon is a third of the Earth's. It is in fact one quarter.

▼WHO FIRST MAPPED THE STARS?

Hipparchus lived on the island of Rhodes in the 2nd century BC, in the eastern Mediterranean. He is most famous for his catalogue of 850 stars observed with the naked eye, which he compiled after seeing an exploding star or 'nova' in the constellation Scorpius in 134 BC. He also devised a system of classifying stars according to their brightness or 'magnitude', still used now.

The magnitude system of Hipparchus divided the stars into six classes, the brightest being magnitude 1, and the faintest magnitude 6. Modern measurements have shown that a 1st-magnitude star is exactly 100 times as bright as one of the 6th magnitude, and on this new scale some stars are rated magnitude 0, or even −1. The brightest star in the sky is Sirius (in the picture), in the constellation of Canis Major (the Greater Dog), which has a magnitude of −1.58. The faintest stars detectable with modern telescopes are about magnitude 24 – 150 million times fainter than the faintest visible with the naked eye!

Hipparchus also developed new ways of measuring the distance to the Moon, and arrived at a result of 30 times the Earth's diameter – extremely close to the true value. He did this by using 'parallax' – measuring the way the Moon seemed to shift in front of the stars as the Earth spun round in space.

Like most of his contemporaries, Hipparchus believed that the Sun and planets revolved around the Earth, and he devised a system of invisible rotating spheres which carried the heavenly bodies.

▶ WHO FIRST SUCCESSFULLY PREDICTED THE MOVEMENT OF THE PLANETS?

Claudius Ptolemy, who lived in Egypt in the 2nd century AD, is most famous for the 'Ptolemaic system' of the Sun, Earth, and planets. He assumed that the Earth was at the centre of the system. To explain the complicated movements of the planets around the sky, he proposed that each planet followed a small circle, or 'epicycle', as it orbited the Earth.

It is amazing that Ptolemy's system, which to us seems completely artificial, allowed the positions of the planets to be predicted so accurately that it was used and accepted for 1,500 years, until the age of modern astronomy began. Ptolemy also produced a revised version of Hipparchus' star catalogue, and gave a list of the 48 constellations recognised in his time. All of these groupings (such as Ursa Major, the Great Bear) are still in use. His observations and catalogue survive in a book called the *Almagest*.

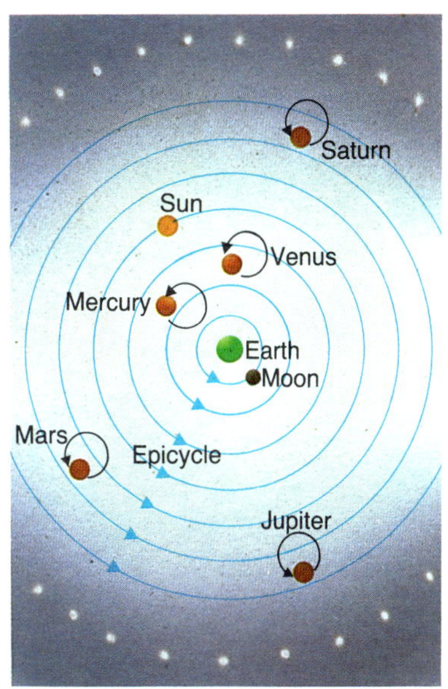

▶ WHO WAS COPERNICUS?

The Polish astronomer Nicholas Copernicus (1473-1543) was the first person since Archimedes to create much interest in the idea that the Earth and planets revolve around the Sun. He published this in a book, the first copy of which he saw only on his death-bed. This book gave the name 'Copernican' to the Sun-centred system.

Copernicus did not propose the modern version of the solar system, since all heavenly motion was believed to be either circular or in a straight line. Since the planets really move around the Sun in ellipses, Copernicus still had to use Ptolemy's epicycles in order to explain their motions around the sky. However, he implanted the idea that the Earth might be moving rather than stationary. For a time, both systems had their supporters.

Copernicus feared disapproval, and stated that the theory was to be thought of as a calculating device, rather than the truth!

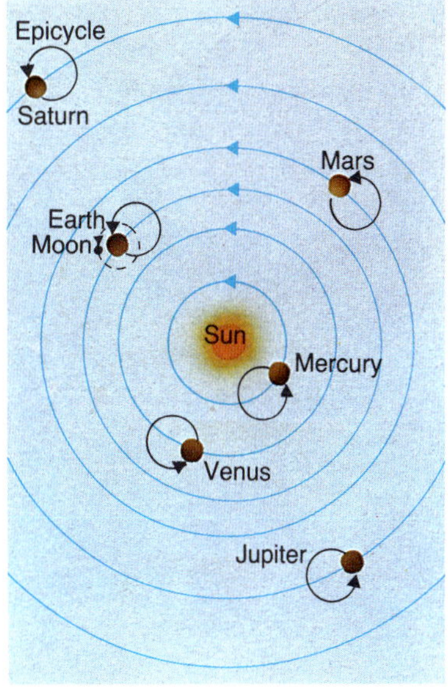

▲ WHO WAS TYCHO?

Tycho Brahe (1546-1601), usually known as Tycho, was the last great astronomer to observe with the naked eye, for the telescope was invented soon after he died. Yet his observations of the planets were so accurate that his successor Kepler used them to prove that the Earth and planets revolve round the Sun.

When he was only 17, the young Dane noticed that the planets Jupiter and Saturn were many degrees away from where the Ptolemaic tables said they should have been. This is what inspired him to make his accurate planetary observations, to establish the basis for the modern theory of the solar system. He didn't fully accept a Sun-centred solar system, so proposed the theory that the planets revolve around the Sun, and the Sun in turn revolves around the Earth. This was to be disproved by Kepler.

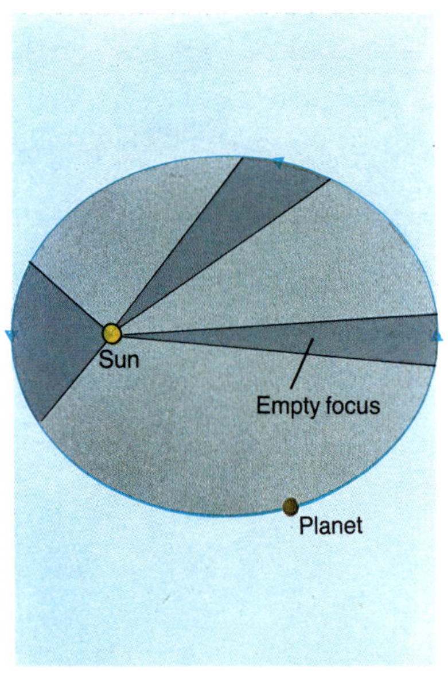

◀WHO DISCOVERED HOW PLANETS MOVE?

Johannes Kepler (1571-1630), discovered the true shape of the planets' orbits around the Sun, which are not circles but ellipses. An ellipse has two points within it, each one called a 'focus'. The Sun is situated at one focus, the other one being empty.

Kepler, who was born in south-west Germany, made his great discovery by using Tycho's observations of the planet Mars. Since he first believed that the planets must move in circles, he spent years trying to make circular orbits 'fit' the observations before abandoning them for ellipses. He also discovered two other laws. One relates each planet's distance from the Sun to the length of its year, and the other states that an imaginary line joining the Sun and a planet will sweep over equal areas in equal times (see illustration), since a planet moves more quickly when at its closest to the Sun.

▶WHO DISCOVERED JUPITER'S MOONS?

Galileo Galilei, who is almost always referred to by his Christian name alone, lived at a very important time for astronomy and science. During his lifetime (1564-1642), the first telescopes were brought into use, and he was one of the first people to point a telescope to the sky, making several very important discoveries.

The Greek philosopher Aristotle had made statements about the natural world which people had, up to the 16th century AD, accepted without question. For example, he had declared that a heavy stone would fall to the ground more quickly than would a light one. There is a legend that Galileo put this to the test, dropping two from the top of the Leaning Tower of Pisa and proved Aristotle wrong, for they both reached the ground at the same time. Although probably untrue, the story highlights Galileo's reputation for a lively and enquiring mind, heralding the modern 'scientific' age.

When news of the telescope's invention reached Italy in 1609, Galileo immediately made himself one, even grinding the lenses, and began making astronomical observations. He saw spots on the Sun, mountains and craters on the Moon, and far more stars than he could see with the naked eye. Turning his instrument to the planets, he saw that Venus shows phases like the Moon and that Jupiter has four bright satellites. He called the satellites the 'Medicean stars', in honour of the Medicis, the ruling family of Florence, where he made these observations.

The phases of Venus proved that it must revolve around the Sun and not the Earth; and the fact that Jupiter had satellites was further proof that astronomical bodies could revolve around objects other than the Earth. However, the Bible was then interpreted as stating that the Earth is the centre of the universe. Galileo, on publishing his discoveries, was accused of heresy, and passed his last years in virtual exile in his villa near Florence.

▲ WHO DISCOVERED URANUS?

William Herschel was one of the greatest astronomical observers of all time. He built the largest telescopes of the age, and discovered the planet Uranus, as well as thousands of new objects inside our own galaxy and other galaxies far away.

Herschel (1738-1822) came to England from his native Hanover to teach music, and began observing in 1774, in his spare time. His discovery of Uranus in 1781 earned him a grant from King George III, permitting him to become a full-time astronomer. He built one telescope with a tube 12 metres long in order to probe as far as possible into space. His main aim was to understand how the stars, star clusters, and clouds of glowing gas revealed by his instruments were distributed in space.

During his researches he discovered more than 800 double stars. He found that some pairs of stars, called binary stars, revolve around each other, taking decades or centuries to do so.

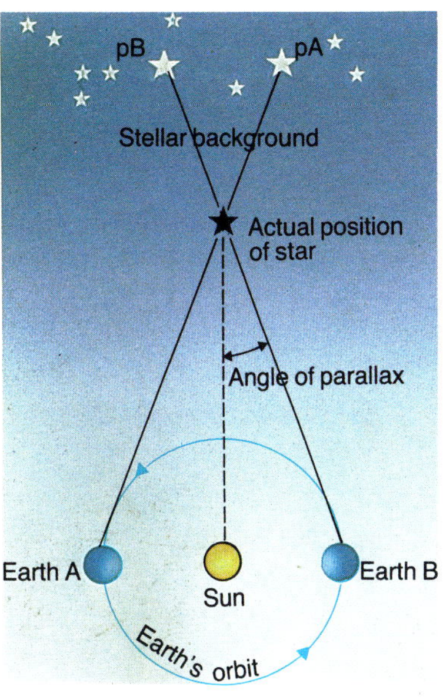

▲ WHO FIRST MEASURED THE DISTANCE TO THE STARS?

Friedrich Wilhelm Bessel (1784-1846), a Prussian astronomer, was the first person to measure the distance from the Earth to a star other than the Sun. This was done in 1838, when he stated that a dim star in the constellation Cygnus lies about 55,000 million kilometres or six light years away.

Bessel achieved this amazing result by using 'parallax'. He observed the star, 61 Cygni, on two nights 6 months apart, so that the Earth was at opposite ends of its orbit. In 6 months the star seemed to move from pA to pB. By measuring the angle of shift (parallax) and the distance from the Earth to the Sun, the distance to 61 Cygni could be calculated.

In 1844, Bessel found that the brightest star in the sky, Sirius, exhibits a very slight and leisurely 'wobble'. He suggested that it was being attracted by an invisible companion revolving around it. This faint star was not seen until after Bessel's death.

▲ WHO WAS HALE?

George Ellery Hale (1868-1938), who began his career as a solar astronomer, is now famous for having planned and built the huge 5-metre aperture telescope on Mount Palomar, California. Completed in 1948, after his death, it remained the world's largest until a 6-metre one was built in the Crimea (Soviet Union) in 1976.

Hale lived at a time when interest in the faint and distant objects of the universe was rapidly increasing. To make them out, telescopes with the largest possible aperture were needed, to collect more light. Four times in his life he built the largest telescope in the world, and all four are still in constant use today. Before the 5-metre he built the 2½-metre and 1½-metre telescopes of the Mount Wilson Observatory, California, all of which use mirrors; and the 1-metre telescope at Yerkes Observatory, Wisconsin, which uses a lens, and has been in operation since 1897.

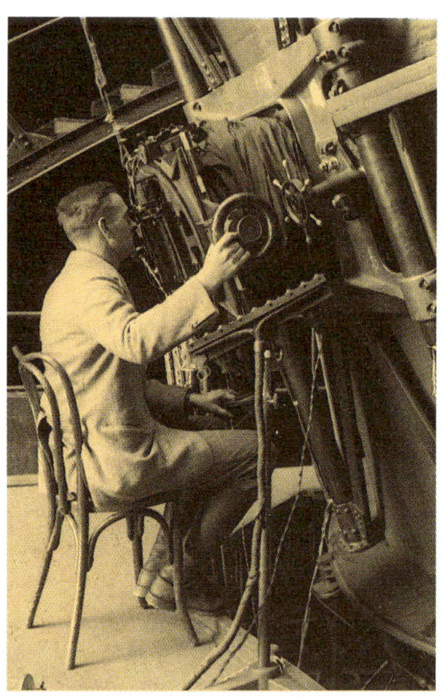

◄WHO MEASURED THE SIZE OF THE UNIVERSE?

The American astronomer Edwin Hubble was the first person to measure the distance to galaxies beyond our own Milky Way. He also suggested that the more distant galaxies are flying away from each other at a greater rate than nearby ones. This is Hubble's Law.

Hubble started his distance measurements by using the largest available telescope (the 2½-metre on Mount Wilson, California) to make out separate stars in the Andromeda galaxy. By measuring how bright they appeared, he could judge how far away they must be. Because of uncertainties about star brightnesses, he obtained a result of 800,000 light-years instead of two million.

Hubble's Law, which states that the speed of a galaxy's flight away from the observer is related to its distance, forms the cornerstone of modern cosmology, for it suggests that all the galaxies were once close together.

►WHO DEVISED THE BIG BANG THEORY?

Abbé Lemaître (1896-1966), a Belgian astronomer, took up the idea suggested by Hubble's observation that galaxies are flying apart. He originated the 'big bang' theory, in which all the material from which the galaxies were formed existed in a single mass or 'cosmic egg', which exploded.

Lemaître's theory is so widely accepted now that it is hard to believe it attracted so little interest when he published it in 1927. The reason is that Hubble's measurements, on which the calculations were based, put the galaxies too close together, which meant that the 'big bang' would have happened only 2000 million years or so ago, making the Universe younger than the Earth!

The breakthrough came during the Second World War. Astronomer Walter Baade (1893-1960) was able to make accurate measurements of galactic distances, and found that the observable universe is much larger than Hubble had

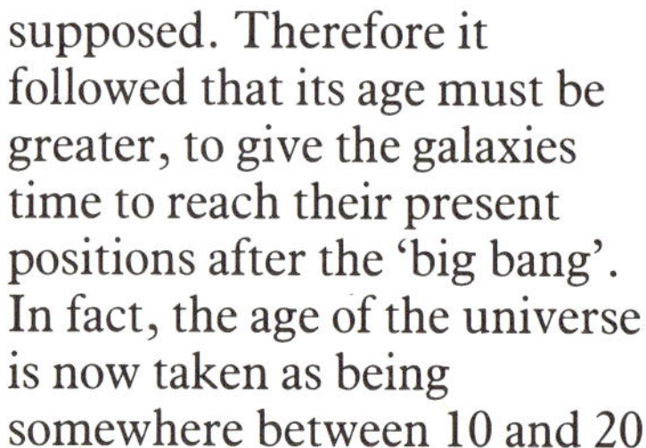

supposed. Therefore it followed that its age must be greater, to give the galaxies time to reach their present positions after the 'big bang'. In fact, the age of the universe is now taken as being somewhere between 10 and 20 thousand million years, far longer than Lemaître's estimate. In that time, if the theory is correct, material thrown out in the explosion has condensed first into galaxy-sized masses, and then into stars within each galaxy.

▼WHO DISCOVERED WHAT STARS ARE MADE OF?

William Huggins (1824-1910) was one of the first astronomers to study the stars using a spectroscope. This is a device which splits light up into its different colours, giving a spectrum. Each element in the universe, when heated, emits light of a certain colour. Therefore, the spectroscope can identify elements in stars.

Huggins was a wealthy amateur, living near London. He made use of the newly-invented photographic process to take photographs of the spectra of bright stars, and compared these with the spectra of elements such as iron, photographed in his observatory, to see if they were present in the stars.

Huggins was one of the first 'astrophysicists' – people who try to understand what stars are made of, and how they shine. He was also able to prove that some stars are flying towards or away from the Sun, by determining changes in their spectra due to this motion.

▼WHO WAS LAIKA?

Laika, a small Eskimo dog, was the first living thing to be sent into orbit around the Earth. She was launched from the Soviet Union in *Sputnik 2* on 3 November 1957. Previously, animals and insects had been launched to high altitudes in rockets, but for only a few minutes.

Laika was launched into an orbit whose altitude ranged from 160 to 1700 kilometres. She was sealed inside a cylindrical chamber about 60 centimetres in diameter, which contained a stock of food and instruments for measuring her heartbeat, breathing, and blood pressure. The reason for the experiment was to see how the strain of take-off and a long period of 'weightlessness' would affect a living creature, before sending a man aloft.

Sputnik 2 fell to its doom on 13 April 1958, but Laika was reported to have been humanely killed long before this. Another animal space pioneer, Ham the chimpanzee, was launched in a brief 'space hop' from Cape Canaveral on 31 January 1961.

▼WHO DISCOVERED QUASARS?

Maarten Schmidt was born in the Netherlands in 1929, and is now Director of the Hale Observatories, California. In 1963 he discovered that the curious 'quasars', or 'quasi-stellar objects', which had baffled astronomers for years, were not stars within our galaxy, but very powerful energy sources at the limit of the observable universe.

These objects had puzzled astronomers because their spectra (the pattern of colours of light they sent out) were different to anything observed elsewhere. Schmidt realised that they were moving away from the Earth at speeds of thousands of kilometres a second, since speed affects the appearance of a spectrum – the so-called 'red shift'.

Following Hubble's Law, Schmidt concluded that the quasars must be more distant than any known galaxies. Physicists have suggested that they are galaxies whose centres are collapsing into a 'black hole', giving out huge amounts of energy.

EXPLORERS AND PIONEERS

▼DID ANCIENT PEOPLE SAIL ACROSS THE OCEANS?

Even without modern navigation aids (such as maps and compasses), ancient seafarers almost certainly made long voyages. Modern explorers have built copies of ancient ships, to prove that such voyages were possible.

In 1947 a balsa wood raft called *Kon-Tiki* sailed across the Pacific Ocean from South America to Polynesia. The leader of the *Kon-Tiki* expedition was a Norwegian called Thor Heyerdahl. He believed that South American people could have crossed the Pacific by raft thousands of years earlier.

In 1969 Heyerdahl set out to prove that the ancient Egyptians could have discovered America 2000 years before Columbus. His international crew sailed a papyrus reed ship, the *Ra* (see picture) from Morocco almost across the Atlantic Ocean.

Other modern seafarers have shown that ancient craft were seaworthy enough to make long voyages. Early explorers must have been just as adventurous as those of today. Some may have been carried far from home by winds or currents. Others may have gone in search of new lands to settle, or just for adventure.

We know that the Vikings sailed to North America around AD 1000. We can be fairly sure that similar voyages had been made thousands of years before.

▶WHO MADE THE FIRST VOYAGES OF EXPLORATION?

The earliest ships were too frail to sail across the open sea. Yet a few brave sailors ventured far from home.

These first explorers kept as close to shore as possible. The Egyptian king Necho II sent a fleet to explore Africa. This was around 600 BC. The Egyptian ships sailed along the east coast and may have got as far as the Cape of Good Hope.

The most famous seafarers of ancient times were the Phoenicians. In 480 BC a fleet of 60 Phoenician ships sailed from Carthage. Their commander, Hanno, led them along the coast of North Africa, visiting Morocco before turning south into the Atlantic Ocean. Hanno may have sailed as far south as Cameroon in West Africa.

The Phoenicians were great traders; among the goods their ships carried was a much-prized blue dye called Tyrian purple.

▼WHO SEARCHED FOR THE LAND OF THULE?

The Mediterranean is a warm, calm sea. The ancient Greeks sailed around it, founding colonies. One bold Greek sailed further, to discover a cold, northern world.

About 300 BC a Greek called Pytheas began a remarkable journey. He lived not in Greece but in the Greek settlement of Marseilles, in France.

He sailed first to Cadiz in Spain, and from there north to Britain. Here he visited the famous Cornish tin mines and explored the country. He worked out the size of Britain fairly accurately and also calculated how far he was from home.

Sailing further north, Pytheas found a cold, icy land. He called it Thule. It may have been Iceland or Norway.

Besides being the first Greek to sail so far north, Pytheas was also one of the first true geographers because he made careful notes of his travels, even describing what the local people ate.

▼WHO WAS CHENG HO?

In the 1400s Chinese ships explored India and Africa. The greatest Chinese navigator was Cheng Ho, whose fleet sailed seas into which no European ships had so far ventured.

The Chinese emperor commanded Cheng Ho to explore the 'western oceans'. From 1405 to 1433 Cheng Ho led seven voyages. His expeditions were on a vast scale: 300 ships carrying 27,000 men.

The Chinese visited Vietnam, Indonesia, Sri Lanka, India, Saudi Arabia and Egypt. They sailed the coast of east Africa. At each place they landed Cheng Ho demanded that the local rulers pay homage to the mighty Chinese emperor.

Cheng Ho's voyages did much to increase China's power and wealth. By the time the first European ships 'discovered' Asia, Chinese fleets had already explored most of the sea routes. Unlike the Europeans, however, the Chinese did not set up permanent trading posts.

▼WHO WAS HENRY THE NAVIGATOR?

A prince of Portugal sent ships to explore distant oceans. He earned the title of Henry the Navigator.

Henry lived from 1394 to 1460. His father was King John I of Portugal. Although he never journeyed far from home, Henry dreamed of exploration and called sailors, map-makers and ship-builders to his palace.

Seeking a new route to Asia, Henry sent ships south, to the unknown coast of west Africa. He encouraged the building of stronger vessels, like the seaworthy caravel, and also the use of improved charts and navigational instruments.

Portuguese ships sent out by Henry discovered the island of Madeira in 1419. Each voyage took them further into the unknown. They landed in Africa, bringing back gold and slaves.

Henry spent so much money backing these voyages that he died in debt. But his dreams had helped to make Portugal one of the great sea powers of Europe.

▶ WHO COMMANDED THE FIRST VOYAGE ROUND THE WORLD?

In 1519 five ships left Spain. Three years later, one returned. It had sailed around the world. The leader of this historic expedition was Ferdinand Magellan. Like most of his seamen, he did not live to see its end.

Magellan was Portuguese and lived from 1480 to 1521. His idea was to sail round South America, and so find a new sea route to Asia. The voyage round Cape Horn was long and perilous. His crew were hungry and sick, and wanted to turn back.

Magellan drove them on, across the Pacific Ocean. The ships reached the Philippines, and here Magellan was killed in a fight with natives.

One ship, commanded by Juan Sebastian del Cano, limped back to Spain. There were 17 Europeans and 4 American Indians on board. Del Cano was greeted as a hero. But it was Magellan's dream that had come true.

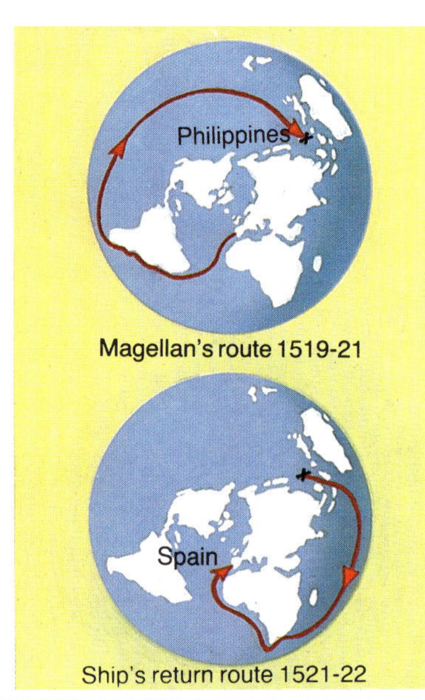

Magellan's route 1519-21

Ship's return route 1521-22

▶ WHICH EUROPEAN SAILOR FIRST REACHED INDIA?

In 1498 a Portuguese named Vasco da Gama arrived in India. Guided by an Arab pilot, he was the first European seaman to land there.

Da Gama left Portugal in 1497 with four ships. As he sailed round Africa, he set up stone pillars to mark each landing place.

The Sultan of Mozambique gave the Portuguese an Arab pilot called Ibn Majid. He knew the Indian Ocean well, and guided the Europeans safely to India. After two years away, Da Gama returned home in triumph.

Vasco da Gama made two further voyages to India and died there in 1524. The Portuguese set up trading posts in India, and Ibn Majid wrote an account of the navigation directions needed to sail across the Indian Ocean.

◀ WHO SEARCHED FOR THE NORTH-WEST PASSAGE?

European merchants dreamed of finding a new, shorter route to Asia. They looked westwards, to the so-called North-West Passage.

By the 1500s many people guessed that the world was round. By sailing *west*, across the Atlantic Ocean, a ship ought to be able to reach Asia.

Even after America was discovered, explorers did not give up this idea. Many seamen tried in vain to find the North-West Passage. Among them were Cabot (1497), Frobisher (1576), Davis (1585), Hudson (1610) and Baffin (1615).

Their sailing ships were not powerful enough to break through the Arctic ice. Henry Hudson died in the search. He was set adrift in a small boat, with his son, when his crew refused to go any further. The North-West Passage was finally navigated in 1906 by the Norwegian Roald Amundsen.

◄WHO FIRST REACHED THE NORTH POLE?

In 1909 two Americans, Robert Peary and Matthew Henson, reached the North Pole. They had made the Arctic journey on foot, accompanied by four Eskimos.

The Arctic is mostly frozen ocean. (The Antarctic is frozen land.) Explorers seeking to reach the North Pole tried to sail as close to it as possible before taking to the ice on foot.

Robert Peary (1856-1920) was a naval officer. He had explored Greenland, learning from the Eskimos how to drive a dog team and how to survive in the Arctic snow and ice.

In 1909 Peary and his five companions set out from Ellesmere Island and succeeded in reaching the North Pole. A rival explorer, Frederick Clark, claimed to have beaten Peary by getting to the Pole in 1908. But today most cxperts agree that Peary deserves the honour of being the first to reach the North Pole.

▲WHICH EUROPEAN FIRST EXPLORED THE SOUTH PACIFIC?

Portuguese, Spanish and Dutch explorers were the first to sail into the vast Pacific Ocean. The greatest of all Pacific navigators was an English captain, James Cook.

Cook was born in 1728. He made three voyages to the Pacific, beginning in 1768. He explored and mapped the coasts of South America, Australia and New Zealand. He even saw the great ice fields of the Antarctic.

He was a brilliant navigator, and was interested in all he saw. He also took care of his crew, making sure his ships carried fresh water, vegetables and fruit to prevent disease. With him on his voyages went scientists, collecting many plants unknown in Europe.

Cook was killed in 1779 by islanders in Hawaii.

►WHO FIRST REACHED THE SOUTH POLE?

Antarctica was the last continent to be explored. In 1911-12 Amundsen beat Scott in a dramatic 'race' to the South Pole.

Two rival expeditions tried to be first to the South Pole: the Norwegians led by Roald Amundsen (1872-1928), and the British, led by Captain Robert F. Scott (1868-1912).

The Norwegians used dogs to haul their supply sledges across the ice. The British, mistakenly as it proved, chose motor sleds and ponies. The motor sleds broke down, and the ponies died.

Amundsen reached the South Pole in December 1911. A month later, Scott arrived to find the Norwegian flag already planted in the snow. Exhausted and short of food, all five Britons died trying to return to their base.

Today, scientists live and work at the South Pole, the coldest and most inhospitable place on Earth.

▶ WHO WAS IBN BATTUTA?

Ibn Battuta was a great traveller. During the middle ages, he visited many lands. He was shipwrecked, crossed the Sahara Desert, and was entertained by kings and princes.

Ibn Battuta was an Arab, born in Morocco in 1304. In 1325 he went as a Muslim pilgrim to Mecca. This was the beginning of his travels, which lasted 30 years and took him an amazing 120,000 kilometres!

He visited Egypt, Africa, Persia (Iran), India, Russia, Mongolia and China. He went wherever there were fellow-Muslims, including Spain (then partly under Moorish rule). Ibn Battuta was a scholar, curious always to know more about new lands. He was famous in his own lifetime, and wrote a book about his travels, describing the Muslim world during the 1300s.

▶ WHICH EUROPEANS FIRST EXPLORED NORTH AMERICA?

Although the Vikings sailed to North America around AD 1000, they did not venture far inland. French traders and explorers were the first to do so, beginning in the 1500s.

In 1534 Jacques Cartier (1491-1557) sailed up the St Lawrence River, and claimed as 'New France' the land we now know as Canada. The French traded with the Indians for furs. One of the most active traders was Samuel de Champlain (1567-1635), who founded settlements at Quebec and Montreal.

French explorers opened up routes westwards and south, into what is now the USA. Robert de la Salle (1643-1687) explored the Great Lakes by boat, and in 1682 he sailed down the Mississippi River to claim the territory of Louisiana for the French king, Louis XIV.

▶ WHO WAS MARY KINGSLEY?

In the 1800s Africa was still wild and unexplored. Few white men had been there, and hardly any white women. Mary Kingsley was one of the first women explorers. Alone, she ventured into West Africa.

Mary Kingsley was born in 1862. At the age of 30, she left her home in England and went to West Africa. She collected insects and fish for the British Museum.

This remarkable woman made several journeys into what was then known as 'Darkest Africa'. She faced many dangers, including cannibals, but showed no fear. She grew to admire the African people she met, and the books she wrote helped people in Europe to understand Africa.

Mary Kingsley died in 1900, nursing in the Boer War. She proved by her expeditions that women could undergo hardship as well as men.

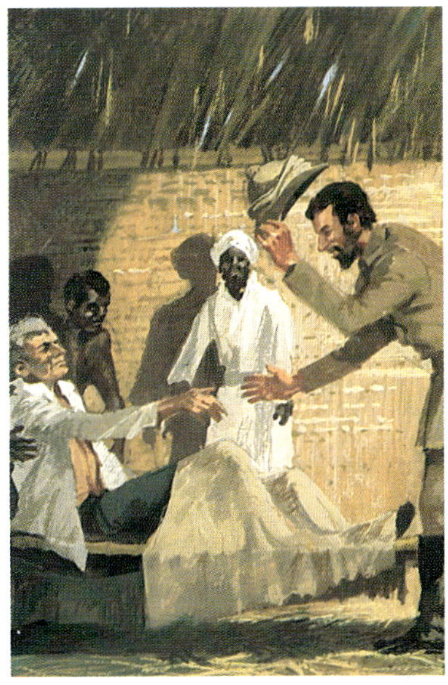

▲ WHO WAS DAVID LIVINGSTONE?

In the 1800s Africa was still largely unexplored. A Scottish missionary named David Livingstone was one of the greatest African explorers. He also did much to end the evil slave trade.

Livingstone was born in 1813. He went to Africa in 1841, to practise medicine and to teach Christianity to the Africans.

Livingstone made several journeys on foot into the unknown heart of Africa. He saw the Kalahari Desert and followed the River Zambezi to discover the magnificent Victoria Falls. Horrified by what he saw of the slave trade, he did all he could to halt it.

In 1866 Livingstone set off to search for the source of the River Nile. Nothing was heard of him until in 1871 an expedition led by Henry Morton Stanley found him near Lake Tanganyika. Though ill, Livingstone went on exploring until he died, in 1873. Two Africans bore his body over 2000 kilometres to the coast, and returned it to Britain.

▲ WHO FIRST CROSSED AUSTRALIA?

Australia was the last continent to be discovered by Europeans. Settlers kept to the coast of Australia, few venturing into the hot, dry interior. In 1861 the first north-south crossing of Australia was made.

The expedition set out from Melbourne. Its leaders, Robert Burke (1820-1861) and William Wills (1834-1861), planned to set up base camps as they travelled. They took camels to carry their supplies.

Four men (Burke, Wills, Grey and King) eventually made the crossing. Weak and ill, they turned for home, but Grey soon died. The return journey took so long that their companions at the base camps gave them up for lost.

When the three survivors reached the Cooper's Creek camp, they found it empty. Burke and Wills both died, and only King was rescued alive by a search party. Wills left a diary, telling of their terrible journey.

▲ WHO WAS ALEXANDER VON HUMBOLDT?

The German scientist and explorer Humboldt travelled in South America. His work was an example to many other geographers.

Humboldt was born in 1769. He trained as an engineer, but in 1799 he went off to South America. With him went his friend, the French botanist (plant expert) Aimé Bonpland (1773-1858).

Humboldt and Bonpland hacked their way through the Amazon jungle and climbed the Andes Mountains. Humboldt kept notes of all they saw, and even recorded what it felt like to suffer from mountain sickness.

After five years, he returned to Europe to teach and write about his travels. He died in 1859. A current in the Pacific, a glacier in Greenland and a river in North America are all named after Humboldt.

▼WHO MADE THE FIRST BALLOON FLIGHT?

In 1783 two Frenchmen rose into the air in a balloon. The age of flight had dawned. The balloon was the invention of the Montgolfier brothers.

Although Joseph (1740-1810) and Étienne (1745-1799) Montgolfier built the first man-carrying balloon, they were not the first air travellers. That honour went to two brave volunteers, J. P. de Rozier and the Marquis d'Arlandes.

The Montgolfiers' balloon relied on hot air (from a fire) for 'lift'. They are said to have thought of the idea from watching smoke rise up inside a chimney.

In 1783 the Montgolfiers amazed the people of Paris by sending aloft a balloon carrying a sheep, a cock and a duck. In November of that year, de Rozier and d'Arlandes made their historic flight, returning safely to Earth and the applause of the huge crowd. Étienne Montgolfier never flew, and Joseph made just one balloon ascent, in 1784.

▼WHO MADE THE FIRST POWERED FLIGHT?

A balloon can fly only where the wind takes it. In 1852 a French aviator tried fitting an engine to a balloon, and succeeded in making the first powered flight.

The aviator's name was Henri Giffard (1825-1882). His 'airship' was a cigar-shaped balloon filled with hydrogen gas for buoyancy. Hanging below it on wires was a flimsy platform which supported a small steam engine. The engine turned a propeller which drove the airship forwards.

The steam engine was too heavy (and dangerous) for Giffard's airship to prove a great success. But it showed the way ahead. It was followed by electrically-driven airships in the 1880s, and later by the huge petrol-engined Zeppelins used by Germany in World War I.

By then airships and balloons had been overtaken by aeroplanes, which flew much faster. However, a few airships can still be seen today.

▲WHO FIRST FLEW FROM FRANCE TO ENGLAND?

In 1909 Louis Blériot (1872-1936), a French pilot, landed his aircraft near Dover. He had made the first-ever flight from France to England.

Blériot became interested in aeroplanes after the Wright brothers' flight in 1903. He built his own aircraft, and his monoplane (single-wing) designs were better than most others of the time. They were light and easy to fly.

A British newspaper offered a £10,000 prize for the first flight between France and England. One of the contestants, another French pilot, crashed into the sea just a few days before Blériot made his attempt.

Without a map or compass, Blériot got lost in mist. His engine overheated, but a rain shower cooled it, and also cleared the mist. Spotting the Dover cliffs below, Blériot flew down to make a rather bumpy landing. His 37-minute flight had made history.

▼WHO MADE THE FIRST SOLO VOYAGE AROUND THE WORLD?

Today, lone sailors often make round-the-world voyages. But in the 1800s such a feat was unknown, until Joshua Slocum showed that it could be done.

Only large sailing ships were thought strong enough to cross the Pacific Ocean and round the stormy seas off Cape Horn, at the tip of South America.

Joshua Slocum (1844-1909) was a Canadian schooner captain. He set out from Boston, USA in 1895 to sail alone around the world. His craft was a small sailing boat called the *Spray*.

The voyage took Slocum three years to complete. Today's ocean racers are much faster, but have automatic steering gear and radar to help them. Slocum relied on his own seamanship and on *Spray*, which he had spent three years rebuilding for the voyage.

In 1909, at the age of 65, Slocum disappeared at sea on his way to South America.

▼WHO WAS THE FIRST WOMAN TO FLY SOLO ACROSS THE WORLD?

In the 1930s many long-distance flying records were set. Amy Johnson was the first woman to fly solo from England to Australia.

Amy Johnson was born in England in 1904. In 1930, only two years after starting to fly, she flew alone in her biplane *Jason* from England to Australia. Flying in stages from one airfield to the next, she made the trip in 19 days.

Another famous airwoman was Amelia Earhart of the USA. She was the first woman to cross the Atlantic by plane in 1928 (as a passenger), and in 1932 she made the first-ever solo Atlantic flight by a woman.

People followed the exploits of these brave pilots on the radio and in the newspapers. In 1937 Amelia Earhart vanished while flying across the Pacific Ocean. Amy Johnson was killed in a plane crash in 1941, while flying for the RAF.

▲WHO MADE THE FIRST NON-STOP FLIGHT ACROSS THE ATLANTIC?

The Atlantic Ocean is over 3,000 kilometres across. Until 1919 no-one had flown across it non-stop. First to do so were two British airmen, Alcock and Brown.

Ocean liners took at least four days to cross the Atlantic. Captain John Alcock (1892-1919) and Lieutenant Arthur Whitten Brown (1886-1948), both RAF pilots, set out to show that an aircraft could make such a long journey non-stop.

They took off in their Vickers Vimy bomber from Newfoundland on June 14, 1919. With the wind behind them, they hoped to reach Europe. Storms and freezing fog threatened the plane, which at one point turned upside-down. After 15 hours, they sighted Ireland and crash-landed into a bog.

They had proved such a flight was possible, and within a few years passenger-carrying planes were making the same crossing.

▶WHO FIRST CLIMBED THE WORLD'S HIGHEST MOUNTAIN?

Mount Everest, in the Himalayas, is the world's highest mountain. No climber had conquered Everest until 1953, when two men at last reached the summit.

The climbers were Edmund Hillary (born 1919) of New Zealand and Sherpa Tenzing Norgay (born 1914) of Nepal. Their expedition was led by John Hunt (born 1910). Six previous expeditions had failed to climb Everest.

Mount Everest is 8848 metres high. The climbers had to carry heavy loads in thin air and freezing cold. They wore special clothing and oxygen breathing apparatus. Hillary and Tenzing were the second pair to try for the summit, after a first attempt failed. On May 29, 1953 they made the last snow ridge and stood for 15 minutes on top of the world.

Since 1953 many other mountaineers have climbed Everest, the peak called by the Tibetans *Chomolungma*, 'Goddess Mother of the World'.

▲WHO PIONEERED DEEP-SEA EXPLORATION?

A human diver cannot go deeper into the ocean than 200 metres or so. Beyond that depth he would be crushed by the pressure of sea water. To explore the seabed people need the protection of special deep-sea submarines. The deepest-diving submarine of all was built by the Piccards of Switzerland.

During the 1930s scientists were lowered into the ocean depths inside a bathysphere. This was a strong steel ball on the end of a long cable. The scientists inside peered out through small windows.

The bathysphere was dangerous (if the cable broke, it was lost) and hard to manoeuvre. So Auguste (1884-1962) and Jacques (born 1922) Piccard, a Swiss father and son team, designed a machine called a bathyscaphe. It worked rather like an underwater balloon. The crew sat inside a round observation chamber under a large float. The float was filled with petrol, and so was lighter than water.

The Piccards built their first bathyscaphe in 1948. To dive, it blew out air from its buoyancy tanks and filled them with water. To rise again, it released metal weights from beneath the body.

In 1960 an improved type of bathyscaphe, called *Trieste*, dived to almost 11,000 metres in the Mariana Trench in the Pacific Ocean. The water here is deep enough to cover the top of Mount Everest! On board were Jacques Piccard and Don Walsh, a US Navy officer.

At such depths, there is no sunlight. The bathyscaphe needed powerful lights to probe the inky blackness. Television cameras filmed strange creatures which live at such depths and which had never before been seen alive.

The bathyscaphe holds the deep-diving record. Other smaller submersibles (diving craft which can go deeper than ordinary submarines) can do useful jobs under the sea. They lay cables and oil pipelines. One day human 'aquanauts' may live for long periods in underwater bases, perhaps farming the fish or digging out valuable minerals from the bottom of the sea.

▲WHO INVENTED THE AQUALUNG?

An aqualung is an underwater breathing apparatus. Wearing it, a diver can swim freely and explore the undersea world. The inventor of the aqualung was Jacques Cousteau.

In the 1930s the French Navy experimented with new types of diving gear for frogmen. Deep-sea divers in their bulky suits with metal helmets could move only very slowly on the seabed, and had to breathe air through hoses running up to the surface.

Jacques Cousteau (born 1910), a French naval officer, wanted to be able to swim freely under water. To do this, he and his team invented skin diving gear and the aqualung. The diver carried air bottles on his back, and swam with flippers on his feet.

Cousteau proved that people could explore and work under the sea. He pioneered the use of special cameras to film the wonders of the ocean. He also built seabed bases for divers to live in.

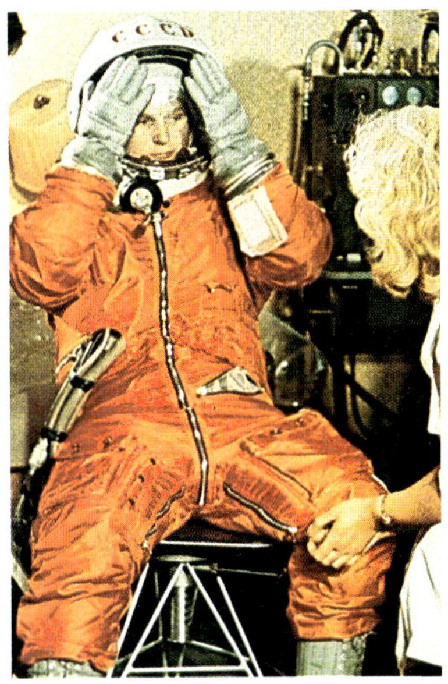

▲WHO WAS THE FIRST WOMAN TO ORBIT THE EARTH?

The first people to train for spaceflight were jet pilots. All were men. But in 1963 a Russian spacewoman made history. Her name was Valentina Tereshkova.

Born in 1937, Valentina started work in a factory. She enjoyed parachuting in her spare time and in 1961 she was accepted for training as a cosmonaut (the Russian term for astronaut).

Even though she was not a trained pilot, Valentina showed great promise. Just two years later, on 16 June 1963, she made her historic space flight. In the spacecraft Vostok 6 she orbited the Earth for 71 hours, returning to a safe landing on 19 June.

Five months after her space flight, Valentina Tereshkova married fellow cosmonaut Andrian Nikolayev. She made no further space flights. But other women, both Russian and American, later followed her example and became astronauts.

▲WHO WERE THE FIRST PEOPLE TO STEP ON TO ANOTHER WORLD?

In 1969 a tiny two-man spacecraft landed on the Moon. Out stepped US astronaut Neil Armstrong to become the first person ever to set foot on another world.

The US Apollo programme, to land astronauts on the Moon, was in response to the Russian success in putting the first man in space (Yuri Gagarin, 1961).

On July 20, 1969 the Apollo programme triumphed. The Apollo 11 spacecraft had been launched from Earth by a giant Saturn 5 rocket. The spidery landing craft settled onto the Moon and Neil Armstrong stepped down onto the surface.

'That's one small step for a man, one giant leap for mankind,' said Armstrong. Fellow-astronaut Buzz Aldrin followed him onto the Moon. Then, rejoining Michael Collins in the waiting Apollo craft above, the pioneers of Moon exploration returned to Earth.

INDEX

Page numbers in italics refer to pictures

PHOTOGRAPHIC ACKNOWLEDGEMENTS

Pages: 12 & 15 bottom right Michael Holford, 22 middle Sonia Halliday, 34 middle Scala, bottom By Gracious Permission of Her Majesty The Queen, 36 top Topham Picture Library, middle Hulton, 40 middle Frank Spooner Pictures, 41 middle Frank Spooner Pictures, bottom Sonia Halliday, 46 top right Ronan Picture Library, 48 top Mansell, 53 top right Hulton, 55 middle Bell Laboratories, 79 bottom right Giraudon, 80 bottom right Simon Warner, The Bronte Society, 83 top right Kobal Collection, 84 top middle, Scala, top right National Gallery, 85 top National Gallery, 86 top & bottom Scala, 87 top left National Gallery, middle Giraudon, right Paul Popper, 89 middle Mansell, 90 bottom left John Topham, right Mander & Mitchenson Collection, 91 bottom The Photo Source, 93 bottom right Mansell, 94 middle Hulton, 95 top middle Mander & Mitchenson, 96 middle Hulton, 97 top Walt Disney Productions Ltd, bottom Paul Popper, 100 top Mansell, 103 top middle Picturepoint Ltd, right Camera Press, 104 bottom left Ronan Picture Library, right Mount Palomar Observatory, 107 top right California Institute of Technology and Carnegie Institution of Washington, 108 top Mount Wilson and Las Campanas Observatory, Carnegie Institution of Washington, 109 bottom left Ronan Picture Library, right Mullard Radio Astronomy Observatory, University of Cambridge, 117 top Mary Evans, 118 top Royal Geographical Society, 119 middle Novosti.
Picture Research: Penny Warn and Jackie Cookson